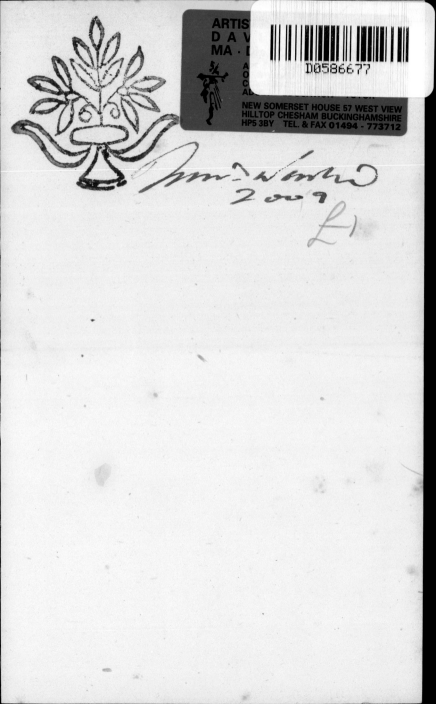

2009

Archæology
and
The New Testament

ARCHÆOLOGY AND
THE NEW TESTAMENT

By

Stephen L. Caiger

*Author of "Bible and Spade," "Lives of the Prophets,"
"The Old Testament and Modern Discovery," Etc.*

*With 8 half-tone plates and
2 maps in text*

CASSELL AND COMPANY LTD.
London, Toronto, Melbourne and Sydney

First Published . . 1939
Second Edition . . 1948

MADE AND PRINTED IN GREAT BRITAIN
AT THE PITMAN PRESS
4.48

PREFACE

In this brief introduction to the study of New Testament archæology I have attempted to write a companion volume to my *Bible and Spade*, which was concerned with the Old Testament only.

The archæology of the Gospels and the early Church bristles with difficulties even more than that of the Old Testament, and different opinions about it are held all the more warmly as the subject is nearer to our hearts. It is certain that the point of view here adopted will not please everyone. But I have tried to give the facts as I know them, together with such sufficient references to other works as will enable the reader to form an instructed opinion for himself.

The scriptural quotations are taken, except where otherwise stated, from the Authorized Version, as the one most likely to be familiar to the general reader, for whom primarily this work is intended.

My grateful acknowledgments are due to the Rev. J. I. Brice, of Cliff College. Calver, for correcting the proofs, and for making many valuable suggestions.

STEPHEN L. CAIGER

Wirksworth Vicarage, 1939.

CONTENTS

LIST OF ILLUSTRATIONS

ARCHÆOLOGY AND THE NEW TESTAMENT

I

THE ARCHÆOLOGICAL APPROACH

A DISTINCTIVELY MODERN CONTRIBUTION

Raise the stone, and there shalt thou find Me : cleave the wood, and there am I.—(A Saying of Christ.)

ALMOST every age has had its own characteristic contribution to make towards the study of the Bible. And every age has been surprised and perhaps a little resentful to find that anything new could be said about a Book so old, and sacred, and already so much discussed. Yet succeeding ages have come to be grateful for the new light thus shed upon the Scriptures, and by its aid have continued to explore still farther afield.

Perhaps the most surprising additions to our knowledge of the Bible are those which have been made within the past century. The true text of the New Testament, for instance, written originally between A.D. 50 and 100, became more accurately known to the critics of the nineteenth century, through the unexpected discovery of long-lost manuscripts, than to any preceding age.

The major triumphs of Textual Criticism, however—crowned by the publication of the Revised Version in 1885

—are now comparatively 'ancient history,' and it would be out of place to dwell upon them here. More recent and more characteristic of the age in which we live is the contribution made by Excavation and the Science of Archæology to the study of the Bible.

It seems strange at first sight that the archæologist should be the last to arrive upon the field of Biblical research. If it seemed incredible that the original text of the New Testament could be discovered after eighteen centuries, how much more fantastic seemed the hope that actual traces or material relics of Bible times and Bible characters might still be discovered beneath the soil of the ages, patiently awaiting the probe of a nineteenth-century spade !

Yet there were reasons why scientific archæology was a practical impossibility at any time previous to the latter years of the nineteenth century. Apart from the fact that the Bible Lands of the Near East—Mesopotamia, Syria, Palestine, Egypt, Arabia, and Asia Minor—were in the possession of governments under which official distrust and popular fanaticism obstructed the work of excavation, our forefathers simply had not the equipment necessary for the task.

An interest in the historical monuments and antiquities of the past had existed, of course, from time immemorial. Greek tourists were scribbling on the pyramids of Egypt in the days of Herodotus (440 B.C.), and hordes of pilgrims followed the Crusaders to the Holy Land in the Middle Ages. But this was not Archæology in any scientific sense. Even the famous *corps des savants* of Napoleon's Egyptian expedition was little more than a party of intelligent sight-seers, compared with the trained experts of to-day.

Only after the invention of certain technical devices, and with the co-operation of many specialists in this or that branch of study, could the significance of those early discoveries be realized, or any real addition to our knowledge of antiquity be made.

The invention of photography, for instance, was an almost indispensable preliminary. It was wonderful what Layard, Niebuhr, Rawlinson and the others managed to accomplish without it, employing artists to sketch the discoveries, taking ' squeezes ' of the inscriptions, or laboriously copying them by hand, making plaster casts, and so on. But such methods involved endless delays and inevitable inaccuracy—to say nothing of real danger to life and limb. To-day the click of a shutter can do in the fraction of a second what the early nineteenth-century archæologist took weeks, months, even years to accomplish, and can do it better. Photography has become the favourite handmaid of modern archæology. Ingeniously devised cameras are sent up in aeroplanes to locate sites buried in desert or jungle, and to detect beneath the grass of featureless pasture-land the faint outline, visible only from a thousand feet above, of deeply-buried emplacements. The infra-red ray has been used to detect long-suspected but hitherto un-proven erasures or corrections in ancient manuscripts. Micro-photography, colour photography, the X-ray, and the ordinary field-camera, all have proved of inestimable service.

Technical devices of every kind have been harnessed to the science. The delicate skill of modern mechanical instruments has made it possible to retrieve what the older archæologist thought for ever lost. Heaps of charred ashes have been reconstructed into legible papyrus scrolls ; a litter of broken earthenware has been rebuilt into a lovely vase ; skeletons ready to fall into dust at the lightest touch have been lifted unbroken from the clay ; chemical re-agents have brought to light inscriptions that had become invisible with age ; and so forth.

The modern archæologist, in fact, shudders to think how many priceless discoveries have been lost to the world for ever, because they were made too soon—too soon for the makers of present-day technique to have used their skill upon them.

So that we are justified in claiming the archæological approach as distinctively modern, the characteristic contribution of our own generation to the study of the Bible.

OLD AND NEW TESTAMENT ARCHÆOLOGY COMPARED

The effect of all this archæological research has been to give the general public a new interest in the Bible. Ever since the discovery, in 1870, of the original Babylonian Flood Story, a steady stream of literature on the subject of Biblical archæology has testified to its wide appeal.

But it is probably true to say that most people have associated the term ' Biblical archæology ' entirely with the *Old* Testament, to the exclusion of the New. This is very evident from the common use of the term ' Bible ' in such book-titles as *The Bible is True*, *The Accuracy of the Bible*, and so on, where it is taken for granted that it refers to the Old Testament alone.

Few readers seem aware of any archæological discoveries bearing specifically upon the New Testament. In all probability, though ' every schoolboy ' has heard of the Flood Line at Ur of the Chaldees, the treasures of Tutankhamen, and the excavation of the walls of Jericho, very few even of his better-informed elders could name a single discovery which has thrown light upon the life and times of Christ, the message of the Gospels, or the history of the earliest Church.

The New Testament archæologist, in consequence, has sometimes almost envied the relative popularity of his Old Testament rival. ' The cuneiform inscriptions have been drawn upon for years by Old Testament criticism,' observes Dr. A. Deissmann, one of the pioneers of New Testament archæology, ' and by a combination of good work and puffery the problem of " the cuneiform inscriptions and the Old Testament " has become so popular, and has been so often handled, that the few scholars who have not yet committed themselves on this question ought really to form an alliance, in order to escape from an isolation that has become almost unbearable ! ' *

Yet the inscriptions of the first-century Roman Empire, and the Greek papyri, recently discovered in Egypt and elsewhere, are as important for the study of the New Testament as the Assyrian or Babylonian records are for the Old. ' Huge as the Old Testament question is, we ought none the less to remember,' continues Deissmann, ' that amid the noise and dust of the great Babylonian work-ground, the age which saw the rise of Christianity has also left written monuments which as a whole possess an importance for the understanding of the New Testament similar to that possessed by the cuneiform inscriptions for the study of the Old Testament, save that the importance does not lie so much on the surface, and is not so easily made plain to every distinguished layman ! '

New Testament archæology, it must be admitted, labours under certain disadvantages as compared with the other. It cannot pretend to make the same immediate appeal to that sheer delight in the gigantic or picturesque which

* A. Deissmann : *New Light on the New Testament*, p. 4.

attracts such crowds to the monuments of Egypt or Mesopotamia. New Testament research has no colossi, sphinxes,
pyramids, or golden coffins to exhibit, nor even mysterious
inscriptions written in unknown tongues.

It must be confessed, too, that there is a romantic glamour
about the antiquities of the very ancient East, surviving so
incredibly from ' the dark backward and abysm of time,'
which few would claim for the pallid ruins of first-century
Asia, Greece, or Rome. Compared with the spacious five
thousand years or more unfolded by the panorama of Old
Testament origins, the three-score-years-and-ten of the
New Testament era seem insignificant, and in point of
fact have inevitably far less to show either in number or
variety of exhibits.

Nevertheless, for the Bible reader who finds in the
Gospel story, rather than in the Law and the Prophets, his
chief spiritual interest, any discoveries which throw light
upon the former must be of paramount importance. It is
helpful and interesting to know about Abraham, Moses,
Sennacherib, and Cyrus ; it is *vital* to know about Jesus
Christ. And if in these latter days we have been given an
opportunity to discover more about the New Testament
through the study of antiquities and the exploration of the
sacred sites, then we should thankfully avail ourselves of it.

The past few decades have, as a matter of fact, witnessed
a great influx of fresh light through the window of archæological discovery ; as in the preceding half-century upon the
Old Testament, so now more particularly upon the New.
So vast is the amount of new material, that even to-day it
has not been thoroughly assimilated, and its full impact
upon the interpretation of the Gospel has yet to be felt.

By the general public its very existence is almost unknown,
for the discoveries have been described for the most part

Plate I

THE WAILING WALL OF THE TEMPLE
The actual stones which Jesus looked upon

(*See page* 68)

only in scattered notices or in publications of a highly technical character. In the present volume, therefore, an attempt is made to give the reader a nodding acquaintance— we claim no more—with the results of archæological research as they bear more particularly upon the life and times and teaching of the New Testament.

SCOPE OF THE PRESENT VOLUME

Everybody knows in a general way what is meant by archæology, but to give a satisfying definition of the word is not as easy as it looks. It may be defined, perhaps, most briefly as the science which deduces a knowledge of ancient times by the search for and study of their existing remains.

It is obvious that such a quest will take us very far afield : the difficulty indeed will be to limit the scope of the enquiry. Many writers proposing to deal solely with ' New Testament Archæology ' have been tempted to follow threads which lead them far beyond the immediate confines of the first century into the endless wilderness of early Christian antiquities, even to the fourth and fifth centuries of our era. Thus the catacombs of the second century, the Palestinian synagogues of the third, the papyri manuscripts of the fourth, and so on, have filled many pages in such books.

The present writer intends to deal sparingly with this sort of material, except in so far as it has a direct bearing upon the New Testament itself, that is to say, upon the actual environment of the first century Roman Empire within which the Gospel of Christ and His Apostles was preached.

Even so, the modern archæologist, thanks chiefly to the excavations of the past seventy years, has an almost in- tractable amount of material to work upon, and material

B

of very different kinds. Everything, strictly speaking, which has survived from the time and place where the New Testament came to birth and was first preached, is grist to his mill—the ornaments, coins, weapons, tools, furniture, utensils, masonry, clothing, pictures, statues, inscriptions, and written documents, which were factors in the everyday life of the period, and of which actual specimens have been found.

The purpose of all this archæological research is not, of course, to fill our museums with pretty or quaint objects of art, nor even to stir our sentimental curiosity about the past. It is to supplement our existing knowledge of the New Testament, gathered chiefly from literature, by the addition of an entirely new source of information, namely, actual visible and tangible remains of the period, supplying details which literature had overlooked or could not possibly have expressed.

Literature at its best can paint but a flat picture of the past. With the aid of archæology we have filled in the background of that picture in a way impossible before. The great figures in the foreground now stand out in stereoscopic clarity, as it were ; we have given them a third dimension.

In our enquiry we shall begin by asking if any actual relics of our Lord Himself or of His Apostles have in fact been preserved, as the piety of past ages has claimed, to give us a clearer picture of them, or to bring us into closer contact with their personalities.

We shall then endeavour to follow in the steps of the Master, tracing His footprints through Jerusalem and the villages of Palestine, and reconstructing in our mind's eye the scene as He saw it, and the surroundings amongst which He moved.

In the same way we shall have to follow S. Paul along the highways of the Roman Empire through Syria, Asia Minor, Greece, and to Rome itself.

The picture would be incomplete unless we accompanied also the humbler disciples of the New Testament Church upon their way, examining such remains as reveal their religious, civic, or domestic circumstances, and the effect of the new Faith upon their manner of life.

Finally, we shall seek for any contemporary or very early Christian writings which may shed new light beyond what is found in the Gospels upon the teaching of our Lord, or bring us nearer to the actual originals of the New Testament manuscripts.

II

PERSONAL RELICS OF CHRIST

Which we have seen with our eyes, which we have looked upon, and our hands have handled, of the Word of Life ; (for the Life was manifested, and we have seen it, and bear witness.)—(I S. John i, 1.)

BEFORE we deal with the excavations, there is one aspect of New Testament archæology which should not, perhaps, be altogether overlooked.

Probably the first question which the ordinary man-in-the-street would ask of the archæologist is : Have you discovered any actual relics of Jesus Himself, or have you found reason to believe that any of the relics claimed as His are genuine ? It is a natural question, and the answer has an interest of its own.

THE TRUE CROSS

The first recorded search for such a relic was due to Constantine, the first Christian Emperor of Rome, by whose orders Jerusalem was explored in A.D. 330 with a view to finding the site of Golgotha and the wood of the True Cross on which Jesus was crucified. Eventually, under the present Church of the Holy Sepulchre a rock-tomb was identified as that of the Saviour, and a wooden beam discovered in a rock-hewn cavity nearby was claimed as part of the original Cross.

According to later legend, three crosses were found, that upon which Jesus had hung being revealed to S. Helena, Constantine's mother, by a miracle of healing.

The occasion has been commemorated in Church calendars ever since A.D. 335 on the Feast of the Invention (Discovery) of the Cross, May 3.

From that date onwards, this wooden beam was venerated in Jerusalem and throughout Christendom as the True Cross itself. In A.D. 614 the Emperor Heraclius, taken prisoner by the Persians, carried it away with him into captivity. But it was later restored to its place of honour in the Holy City. During the Middle Ages splinters of this Holy Rood were taken away by pilgrims as souvenirs, until it is said ' there were enough pieces of the True Cross in England alone to build a battleship ! ' To this day little crosses are procurable professing to contain tiny fragments of the sacred wood. And thousands of people, without any idea of why they do it, ' touch wood ' to avert ill luck. Of all the so-claimed relics of Christ, these pieces of the True Cross have thus as respectable a pedigree as any.

But it is obvious at once that this is not saying much. There are too many gaps even in this ancient chain. It is not, of course, *impossible* that the wood of the actual Cross of Calvary might still have been in existence for Constantine to discover three centuries after the Crucifixion, especially as it was in a dry stone cavity or cistern that the discovery was made. Nor is it *impossible* that the wood which Heraclius carried away with him, or the wood which was restored to Jerusalem in A.D. 614, or the splinters which the pilgrims brought to Europe in the Middle Ages, belonged in actual fact to the same piece of timber which Constantine found in A.D. 330.

But it is so palpably impossible to prove even the probability of such being the case, that the scientific archæologist refuses to consider the question. He neither denies nor affirms.

PORTRAITS OF CHRIST

The same is true of the many representations of one kind or another which have been claimed as authentic contemporary portraits or ' true likenesses ' of Christ.

From very early days lovers of the Lord Jesus have wanted to know just what He really looked like as He went about doing good. Was He tall or short, dark or fair, bearded or shaven ? What sort of eyes were they which with one glance could drive away suffering, or make men follow Him to their lives' end ?   Surely some contemporary picture, carving, or detailed representation of Him had survived to help one visualize Him as He appeared to the multitude when Pilate said, ' Behold the Man ! '

It was a natural craving, and many attempts have been made to satisfy it.

THE TIBERIUS GEM

One of the most beautiful of such portraits of Jesus is that which claims with some particularity to be *A True Likeness of Our Saviour, copied from the portrait carved on an emerald by order of Tiberius Cæsar, which emerald the Emperor of the Turks afterwards gave out of the treasury of Constantinople to Pope Innocent VIII for the redemption of his brother, taken captive by the Christians.*

On the reverse of this portrait, still frequently reproduced in answer to popular demand,* one reads a description of our Lord supposed to be ' copied from an original letter written by Publius Lentullus, President of Judæa in the days of Tiberius Cæsar to the Roman Senate,' as follows :—

> *He was a man of stature somewhat tall and comely, with very reverend countenance, such as the beholders may both*

* It may be purchased from most Roman Catholic booksellers.

*love and fear. His hair is of the shade of a chestnut full-
ripe, plain to His ears, whence downward it is more orient
and curling and waving about His shoulders. In the
midst of His head is a seam or partition in His hair, after
the manner of the Nazarites. His forehead plain and very
delicate ; His face without spot or wrinkle, beautified with
a lovely red ; His nose and mouth so formed as nothing can
be reprehended ; His beard thickish, in colour like His hair,
not very long but forked. His look innocent and mature ;
His eyes grey, clear, and quick. . . .   In proportion of body,
excellent. His hands and arms most delicate to behold.
A man for His singular beauty surpassing the sons of men.*

It is such a picture of Jesus as a saint might see, dreaming
of Him on his knees. As a ' True Likeness ' of Him it is
in a sense truer than the truth, for the eye of the soul has
seen something that no eye of flesh could have perceived.
But it is very obviously *not* the description which a Roman
' President,' or any other Roman of the days of Tiberius
Cæsar, would have written. On the contrary, it breathes
in every word the spirit of comparatively sophisticated
piety, and is clearly based on typical representations of our
Lord such as were painted by the old Masters.

Examining the portrait to which the above description is
attached in the cold light of archæology, its claim to be
copied from an emerald intaglio ' executed at the order
of Tiberius Cæsar, etc.' cannot be sustained.

It is true that early second-century examples of Christian
inscriptions in intaglio have been found, cut on jewels of
jasper, onyx, emerald, chalcedony, and so forth for use in
signet rings. But in the earliest gems our Lord is represented only under the form of emblems such as the dominical
monogram IHC or XP, or the mystic FISH (the Greek

letters of which ($I\chi\theta\nu\varsigma$) stand for ' Jesus Christ the Son of God our Saviour ').* Later on He is represented conventionally in the form of the Good Shepherd, the earliest example of this occurring at the end of the second century. It is only from the fourth century and onwards that an attempt is made to portray His actual countenance in this medium.

According to the Dictionary of Christian antiquities, the so-called ' Emerald of Tiberius ' (which is now lost but was once among the treasures of the Vatican) ' was probably a plasma of the early Byzantine School '—that is to say, it emanated from the Eastern Roman Empire of Constantinople, some four centuries later than the time of Tiberius Cæsar.

The intrinsic beauty and spirituality of the portrait, however, must have been considerable, for it greatly influenced the earliest mediæval paintings of our Lord, and established a kind of standard portrait of Him even to this day. Actual copies made from this gem, dating from the sixteenth century, still exist.

But the modern engravings and photogravures of this ' True Likeness of Our Saviour ' are not direct reproductions even of these copies. Actually, they are more or less faithful copies of the Head of our Lord in Raphael's beautiful picture of the Miraculous Draught of Fishes, painted in the sixteenth century—which, however, may have owed some of its inspiration to the Gem.†

OTHER ' PORTRAITS '

The claim of other paintings to be contemporary pictures of our Lord or His friends falls equally to the ground.   In

* F. W. Farrar : *Christ in Art.*
† *Dictionary of Christian Antiquities*, Vol. I, p. 718.

the Church of Santa Maria Maggiore in Rome, for example, is a very ancient portrait of the Blessed Virgin Mary ascribed to S. Luke the Evangelist. But its history can be traced no farther back than A.D. 847.

The tradition that S. Luke was a painter of portraits is, indeed, much older than that. It first appears in the pages of one Theodore Lector, writing in the sixth century, who states that the Empress Eudoxia found at Jerusalem about A.D. 460 a picture of the Mother of Jesus which was immemorially believed to have been painted by S. Luke. But the pedigree of the picture now shown as such goes back no farther than A.D. 1200, when it was brought to Venice by the Crusaders.

THE CATACOMB PORTRAITS

Undoubtedly the earliest portraits of our Lord or His Saints are those which may still be seen in the celebrated Catacombs in Rome, those labyrinthine underground passages beneath the city where the early Christians secretly buried their dead, covering the stone walls with paintings, inscriptions, and other marks.

The date of the earliest markings left by Christians upon the catacomb walls is uncertain. Some of them are believed to be as old as the end of the first century of our era, and may therefore be the work of men who had actually seen the Lord. But among these earliest wall-markings there are no true pictures, only roughly executed emblems and inscriptions.

The earliest pictures of Christ in the catacombs are obviously not intended as portraits at all, but rather as conventional representations of His Divine personality. Many of them are Christian adaptations of the pagan art so well known from excavations at Pompeii and Herculaneum.

Sometimes the figure of the Saviour is merely a variation of familiar pictures of Cupid or Adonis !*

More frequently He is portrayed as the Hermes or Mercury of the new Faith, or as a beardless youth clad in the usual dress of a Roman shepherd-boy carrying a lamb or two on His shoulders, a staff in His hand, and followed by His flock.

In some of the earliest of these pictures of the Good Shepherd He is shown carrying not only a lamb, but what is apparently intended as a kid or a goat in His arms—as noted by Christina Rossetti in one of her most touching sonnets :—

> Then smiled the Church ; and in the Catacombs,
> With eye suffused but heart inspirèd true,
> On those walls subterranean, where she hid
> Her head mid ignominy, death and tombs,
> She her Good Shepherd's hasty image drew—
> And on His shoulders, not a lamb—a kid !

At a later date, He is still represented quite without any attempt at realism, sometimes as very young with His disciples like children around Him, and sometimes as a bearded old man with His twelve Apostles looking like venerable Roman senators.

It is clear, as Cobern observes, that ' in the earliest pictures there is no attempt at making a likeness of the Saviour, the conception being purely ideal, representing a beardless youth in the serene joy of a noble and divine task.'†

In many parts of Christendom, in fact, the attempt to portray the features of Christ was viewed with distrust and generally discouraged. Not only did the old Jewish

---

* The features of Phidias' celebrated Olympian Zeus may also have influenced early Christian artists.
† C. M. Cobern : *The New Archæological Discoveries*, p. 395 f.

prejudice against ' graven images ' still linger, but Gnostic
heretics had made a practice of painting entirely imaginary
portraits of Him, and then claiming them as authentic.
Amongst other early Fathers of the Church, S. Augustine
(c. A.D. 400) comments unfavourably on the dangerous
device of ' inventing portraits of the Lord Himself in the
Face of His Flesh, each as different from the other as the
opinions of their inventors.'

There is, in fact, no record amongst early Christian
writers of the existence of an authentic or contemporary
portrait of Christ.

Not until the middle of the fourth century does a new
tendency appear to modify the hitherto conventional portraits
of Christ by introducing distinctive personal characteristics,
and the semblance of realism. Now for, perhaps, the
first time it occurs to the catacomb artist that Jesus was not
after all a Roman Citizen like himself, but a Jew of Palestine,
and the attempt is made to portray Him as an Oriental, clad
in the flowing robes of the East.

From about this time forward the representation of the
face of Jesus which is now familiar to us all becomes almost
a fixed convention. He wears a short beard ; His brow is
broad and calm, shaded by long brown hair parted in the
middle and falling to the shoulders in a gentle curl ; His
eyes are large and thoughtful.

Perhaps the most ancient example of this type of portrait
may be seen in the fresco painted on the ceiling of the
catacomb of S. Domitilla. It will be seen from the accom-
panying photograph (Plate II) that it has not yet attained the
gentleness and beauty of later developments, but has a
certain quiet dignity and attraction of its own. It represents
the head of our Lord in profile, with a short chin beard
and moustache, and dark longish hair. The brow is noble,

the aquiline nose well proportioned. One shoulder is bare, the other covered by a toga.

The catacomb of S. Domitilla is one of the earliest, possibly as early as the first century, but this of course is not to say that all the wall-paintings found in it were of the same date. The catacombs continued in use for centuries, and Christian piety was continually adding to their adornment. According to most authorities, this so-called 'Prototype Portrait of Christ' is probably not older than the fourth century.

A fairly safe criterion of date is the presence or absence of the nimbus or halo which from the fourth century onwards began to crown the head of the Saviour, the Blessed Virgin, and ultimately all the Saints of the Church. One of the earliest pictures of the Madonna, for instance, is the famous Virgin and Child from the catacomb of S. Priscilla, where neither she nor the Holy Child has the halo around the head. She is clothed, too—another sign of early date—in the ordinary robe of a Roman maiden, the Babe lying naked in her arms.

Yet another mark of comparatively early date is the absence of any sign of suffering upon the countenance of the Saviour. It is only after the fourth century that we find portraits, like that on the legendary Handkerchief of S. Veronica, showing Him as the Man of Sorrows and acquainted with grief, His haggard features drawn with pain, while drops of red blood fall from the Crown of Thorns about His brow. The Crucifix, in fact, is many centuries later than the empty Cross.

THE SHROUD OF TURIN

Mention of the Handkerchief of S. Veronica reminds us of a custom which prevailed in the Roman Church in the first few centuries, of covering the faces of the dead with portraits of Jesus painted upon linen.

In the Church of S. Prassedes in Rome there is a linen portrait of this type, which is said to have been painted by S. Peter at the request of Prassedes and Pudentiana, daughters of Pudens and Claudia, and to have been preserved by S. Helena, mother of Constantine, in its present casing of silver and enamel !

But the most celebrated portrait of Jesus on cloth is the beautiful ' Shroud of Turin,' an oblong, grey-white, linen sheet, upon which can be discerned the shadowy outline of a human body lying at full length as though in the hour of death. Upon this outline, in the exact position of the Five Wounds of the Redeemer—His hands and feet and pierced side—are dark stains as of blood. The shadows which compose the head and face, rather after the style of a photo-graphic negative, yield a positive print showing features of a remarkable beauty and nobility. It is sometimes claimed as the actual shroud in which the Saviour's bleeding body was wrapped for the Burial.

This relic has been subjected to various scientific tests, and the question of its authenticity has been seriously discussed by leading French *savants*. It is something of a mystery how the impression of a human figure has been produced upon the linen, for photo-micrography shows it not to have been *painted* or *drawn* upon it. The markings have been chemically produced in just such a manner, it is said, as would be caused by the aloes of anointing and ammonial exhalations from a corpse. There is no record, however, that modern blood-tests have been applied to the ' stains made by the wounds.'

Perhaps one should add that a Papal Bull of Clement VII forbade the exhibition of this shroud as an authentic relic of Christ, though it is still taken out of its silver casket from time to time, unrolled behind the Cathedral altar, and shown with great ceremony to the people.

That the shroud may indeed have covered a wounded corpse, and that the impression upon it might have been caused as suggested above, is not impossible. But it can scarcely have been the Shroud of Christ. Judging by the Scriptural records, His body was wrapped in a kind of winding cloth, rather than covered by a shroud, with a separate binder enfolding His head. When Peter descended into the Holy Sepulchre after the Resurrection he saw ' the napkin that was about His head, not lying with the linen clothes, but wrapped together in a place by itself.' (S. John xx, 7.)

Nor can the pedigree of the shroud be traced farther back than the fourteenth century, when, like so many other relics, it was brought by the Crusaders from the East. It remained for many centuries the property of the House of Savoy, but is now in the custody of the Cathedral of Turin.*

PORTRAITS OF THE APOSTLES

The earliest fresco of Christ surrounded by His Apostles, painted with any attempt at distinctive portraiture, appears in the catacomb of S. Domitilla, and dates about the fourth century. Curiously enough, in the earliest pictures there is more character about the portraits of S. Peter and S. Paul than about those of our Lord. It is almost as though some recollection of these two great Apostles, at one time resident in Rome, had in truth lingered on for future generations to recall and to delineate.

From the first S. Peter is clearly distinguished from

---

* For an appreciative account of this relic see A. S. Barnes: *The Holy Shroud of Turin*, and K. Proszynski: *The Authentic Photograph of Christ*.

S. Paul, and there is a continuous persistence of type in their portraits. S. Peter has a short beard and close curly hair, while S. Paul is painted with a long pointed beard and a bald head. Many scholars think it possible that this tradition goes back to the Apostles themselves. ' There is no doubt,' declares Professor Lanciani, ' that the likenesses of S. Peter and S. Paul had been carefully preserved in Rome ever since their lifetime. These portraits have come down to us by scores. The type never varies. S. Peter's face is full and strong, with short curly hair and beard ; while S. Paul appears more wiry and thin, slightly bald, with a long pointed beard. The antiquity and genuineness of both types cannot be doubted.'*

The ' scores of portraits ' to which the Professor refers have been found not only painted upon the walls of the catacombs, but engraved on brazen medals, cut on jewels, embossed in silver, and outlined in enamel and gold medallions on the bottom of gilded drinking glasses, of which a large number have been found in Rome. The date of these portraits, however, has been fixed at the late second and early third centuries, so that none of them is actually contemporary with the New Testament period.

VISUALIZING CHRIST

The quest for an actual well-authenticated contemporary portrait of Jesus or any of His disciples has resulted, therefore, in disappointment. It would require the very strongest evidence to convince a modern archæologist that any supposed picture of this kind was a genuine product of the first century.

On à priori grounds, the notion that a contemporary artist would engrave or paint His features is unlikely. In

* R. Lanciani : *Pagan and Christian Rome*, p. 212.

His lifetime all His admirers were either Jews like Himself, or under the influence of Jewish modes of thought, and would have been horrified by representations of human features, especially those of the Messiah.*

Moreover, the itch to preserve and venerate relics did not exist in the first century. It is in the highest degree unlikely that anybody in the multitude which saw Christ crucified would have dreamed of taking away with him a souvenir of the occasion, such as the hammer, the nails, the hyssop-rod, the crown of thorns, or chips from the Cross, in the way that a twentieth-century spectator might do.

Nor were men interested in those little personal and intimate details which loom so large in modern hero-worship. The literature of antiquity in general, and the Bible in particular, is singularly silent on such points. Throughout the whole of the Old and New Testaments, for instance, it would be difficult to find a case where a man's features or personal appearance are described in any detail.

Not till the end of the second century do we come across an attempt at a personal description, such as that of S. Paul in the spurious *Acts of Paul and Thecla* : *He was a man of small stature, almost bald, bandy-legged, of full habit, with eyebrows joining, and a hooked nose.*

It is unlikely, then, that our attempt to visualize Jesus as He really was will receive any help from contemporary or first-century paintings, drawings, sculpture, or literary descriptions. So far nothing of the sort has been discovered, and scientific archæology must perforce remain silent on the subject.

We may speak, perhaps, with rather more confidence about the *general* appearance of Jesus and His disciples—

---

* This was probably true of the Jews of the first century of our era, in spite of the later elasticity on the point (see p. 84ff).

Plate II

THE EARLIEST PORTRAIT OF CHRIST
From the Catacomb of Domitilla
(*See page* 17)

THE WIEGAND CUP
Jesus may have used a cup like this
(*See page* 29)

the fashion in which they dressed their hair, the clothes they wore, and so on. In the proverbially 'unchanging East' there has been (until recently) a fixed custom in such respects, and several hints in the New Testament narrative suggest that a reconstruction on these lines may be near the truth. That there was nothing markedly out of the ordinary in our Lord's physical appearance seems to be shown by the necessity that Judas should point Him out from amongst others in the Garden of Gethsemane, as well as by other incidents in His life. And nowhere do we find a hint that the Apostles were distinguished by any outward mark of dress.

To take one obvious point: from the earliest times the Jews of Palestine have been accustomed to wearing beards. They are so represented on Egyptian and Assyrian pictures many centuries before Christ, and subsequent representations show that as a people they never departed from the custom. It is true that in our Lord's day many upper-class Jews of Hellenistic or Roman sympathies went clean-shaven as an outward sign of their broad-mindedness, but our Lord and His Judæan fishermen would hardly be of the number. So that in this respect the traditional portrait of Jesus is probably correct.

The same cannot be said of the standard conception of His style of dress. By analogy we may assume that His vesture was not very different from that worn to-day by the older and more conservative Jews of Palestine, which has certainly a tradition of many centuries behind it.

A writer who can be trusted on this subject thus describes Him as He most probably appeared: 'Upon His head He must have worn the turban, the national headgear, used alike by rich and poor. Painters make a mistake when they represent Christ as bare-headed. . . . Under His turban

c

He wore His hair rather long and His beard uncut. His tunic and underneath vesture was of one piece without seam. Over this He wore the *talith* loose and flowing. Possibly it was blue, for blue was then very common, or it may have been simply white with brown stripes. He wore sandals on His feet, as we learn from John the Baptist ; and when He was travelling from place to place He doubtless wore a girdle round His loins.'*

Beyond this we cannot go. And what has been said about Jesus was probably true of His twelve Apostles as well. They were men of their time and clime. Of the later New Testament characters, who shed to a certain extent their early Judaism in favour of a more Catholic outlook, we cannot be sure. But it seems probable that many of them, including Paul the ' Roman Citizen,' would adopt the more convenient and less conspicuous garb of the ordinary Roman traveller.

THE HOLY GRAIL

Very dear to the heart of the romantic Middle Ages was the hope of finding the long-lost ' San Greal ' (originally *Sang Real*, Holy Blood) or ' Holy Grail,' that is to say the actual Chalice which Jesus used at His Last Supper with the Apostles in the Upper Room :—

> The cup, the very cup from which Our Lord,
> Drank at the last sad supper with His own.
>
> *Tennyson.*

According to a mediæval legend, the Holy Grail was brought by Joseph of Arimathea to Glastonbury where maybe it still remains for some fortunate archæologist to unearth. In his brochure on the subject, Dr. Rendel

---

* D. Stapfer : *Palestine in the Time of Christ.*

Harris remarks : ' I notice that so careful an antiquary as Mr. Arthur Weigall (the noted Egyptologist) regards the excavation of the Cup as a possibility. One can believe anything at Glastonbury and in the Glastonbury atmosphere.'*

THE GREAT CHALICE OF ANTIOCH

A claim that it is the actual Holy Grail used by Our Lord at the Last Supper has recently been made, and with some show of archæological research, on behalf of the so-called ' Great Chalice of Antioch,' an article of undoubted antiquity and considerable beauty now in the United States.

A detailed description of this Chalice, together with exquisite photographs, may be found in Dr. G. A. Eisen's mammoth-size two-volume treatise,† which may be consulted in the British Museum. It is the only account authorized by the owners of the Chalice, Messrs. Kouchakji of New York.

This celebrated ' chalice ' is a silver cup or beaker, standing about five inches high, slightly tapering towards the base, and made to be lifted to the lips without a handle. It is covered with an ornamental design of exquisite workmanship engraven and deeply chased in the metal.

The general design of the ornamentation is a vine with many intertwining leaves and bunches of grapes springing from six pairs of stems. Within the enfolding leaves of the vine are twelve medallion-like spaces, each of them containing a human figure, usually seated, and delineated in careful detail. The six figures on one side of the cup represent Christ as a young man surrounded by five adoring Apostles. The six figures on the other side represent

* R. Harris : *Glass Chalices of the First Century*, p. 3.
† G. A. Eisen : *The Great Chalice of Antioch*.

Christ as an older man again surrounded by five Apostles. The symbolism in general is clearly ' eucharistic,' that is to say, connected with the Holy Communion. In one relief Christ points to a plate with seven loaves and two small fishes. In another, a lamb looks up at Him. In another, we see a basket of loaves and grapes surmounted by a winged eagle.

Of the portraits so engraven, Dr. Eisen writes : ' The face of the Christ seems divine ; no subsequent artist has succeeded in imparting that sweetness and gentleness which tradition gives to the Saviour's features, and which we have for the first time seen realized. The heads of the Apostles are equally remarkable. We seem to read the character of each of them ; the very soul of man is here portrayed in the metal as, perhaps, never before or after in Christian art.' He claims, in fact, that the portraits on this chalice are actually contemporary representations of our Lord and His Apostles, or at least that they were engraved before A.D. 64 by an artist who had seen the Lord.

But Dr. Eisen makes a still more ambitious claim for his chalice. It is a remarkable fact that the exquisite and costly silver exterior described above is not, apparently, the original chalice, but is an ornamental container, so to speak, holding within it an older and plainer drinking cup. This inner bowl is of quite trivial value and inferior workmanship.

The suggestion is that this humble inner cup must have had some peculiarly sacred associations about it, causing it to be preserved as a relic, and afterwards enshrined in the elaborate casing which we admire to-day. Dr. Eisen, in short, confidently identifies the inner bowl of the Great Chalice of Antioch as the long-lost Holy Grail itself. And he has not been altogether without learned support for his thesis. Generally speaking, however, expert opinion has tended to throw very cold water over it.

Again, the pedigree of the chalice, as so often in such cases, is highly unsatisfactory. Dr. Eisen can give no real account of the circumstances under which it was found. It was put up for sale at Antioch in Syria by some Arabs, but it is admitted that ' they refused to reveal the exact site of their discovery.'* It is questionable, in fact, whether it was found at Antioch at all, so that its association with the city ' where the disciples were first called Christians ' may be quite fortuitous.

As to the age of the chalice, Dr. Eisen would ascribe it to a date before A.D. 64, basing his opinion on the presence of the eagle among the engraved figures. ' The eagle being the official emblem of the Roman government, which after Nero's persecutions in A.D. 64 became naturally anathema to Christians, would scarcely have been allowed upon a Eucharistic chalice.' It is as though one were to argue that all eagle lecterns in English churches must be earlier than 1914, because in that year the eagle became an emblem of a hostile Power through the Great War ! In any case, the Imperial Eagle was presumably restored to favour when the Emperor Constantine became a Christian soon after A.D. 300. So that the same argument might as easily be made to prove a fourth-century as a first-century date for the chalice.

As a matter of fact, it is to a date in the fourth or fifth century at the earliest that the majority of serious archæologists attribute this interesting object. In the first place, the Arabs who offered it for sale in Antioch produced at the same time some other articles—a silver cross, three ornamental book-covers, and a second chalice—all apparently

* A deadly attack on Dr. Eisen's theories will be found in D. Jerphanion : *Le Calice d'Antioch* (1926).

discovered in the same cache, and all indisputably belonging to the fifth or sixth centuries.

Artistically, too, the ornamentation on the chalice has distinct affinities with fifth-century Byzantine work. The *motif* of medallions enclosed in an inflorescence of vine leaves and grapes is characteristic of this period, and in the case of the chalice is in precisely the same Hellenistic style as the ivory pyxes of Bobbio.* Sir M. Conway (later Lord Conway of Allington), an authority on such matters, declared roundly : ' It is not in work produced at Byzantium, but rather in the ivories and sculptures that came out of the workshops of Egypt, the Levant and Asia Minor, that we must seek for its origin.' He compares it with the eighth-century Ivory Throne at Ravenna, and with many examples of foliated figures in Coptic galleries in Cairo Museum. His conclusion—with which the British Museum experts agree—is that the chalice is of mid-sixth-century workman-ship.†

Finally, a dispassionate examination of the exquisitely-clear photographs reproduced in Dr. Eisen's treatise fails utterly to perceive in the portraits of Christ and His Apostles (if so they be—there are only *ten* of them !) that perfection of beauty or individuality of which he speaks so enthusi-astically. The figures are all, to tell the truth, very similar to one another, and in every case the faces are indistinct, *and the noses completely rubbed off !*

In short, one fears that the ' Great Chalice of Antioch ' must go the way of all the other so-called relics of Christ. It cannot be seriously claimed as contemporary, nor as perpetuating a ' true likeness ' of the Saviour of the World, nor yet as preserving the authentic Holy Grail.

* J. Dalton : *East Christian Art* (1925).

† M. Conway in *Burlington Magazine*, Sept., 1924, p. 105.

THE WIEGAND CUP

We are now able, however, to conjecture with some approach to probability just what the Holy Grail would look like if and when it were found, for several typical drinking cups have been discovered, such as were used by the humbler classes of Palestine in the first century of our era.

They are made of glass, with a homely Greek inscription running round the bowl.

One of them, the Wiegand Cup (plate II), is particularly interesting in this connection, for the inscription which encircles it is the favourite and most commonly chosen of all such drinking-cup inscriptions, and therefore has the best chance of being that used in the Holy Grail. It runs :

What are you here for ? Cheer up !

’εφ’ ὃ πάρει ; εὐφράινου

Deissmann* goes so far as to detect a subtle reference to this inscription in the Gospel of S. Matthew (xxvi, 50), where our Lord addresses these very words to Judas at His betrayal in the Garden of Gethsemane : ‘ Comrade, *what are you here for ?* ’ ἑταῖρε, ’εφ’ ὃ πάρει ;—a somewhat unusual phrase, except on such cups. It is as though our Lord were reminding the Traitor of the ‘ Cup of Kindness ’ they had so lately shared together.

There are now about half a dozen of these inscribed glass cups of the first century on view in various collections. They all exhibit the ‘ What-are-you-here-for ? ’ legend, and are all without stems and without handles. Some of them are shaped exactly like the ‘ Coronation beakers ’ familiar to every English child. A more or less elaborate pattern runs in relief around the bowl between heavily-moulded parallel rings.

* A. Deissmann : *Light from the Ancient East* (1927 ed.), p. 125.

Dr. Rendel Harris* gives some very interesting quotations showing the continued use of similar glass cups at the Eucharist in later years. In the third century a certain Epimachus writes : ' As for the vessels wherein we are given Communion, they are of glass, for we be poor men, dwelling in a tiny hamlet.' In the eighth century, again, the Patriarch Alexander II writes : ' We have made, instead of gold and silver, cups of glass and patens of wood.' Similar instances could be multiplied from the poverty-stricken Mission Field of to-day.

The first Lord's Supper belonged to the ' Silver-and-gold-have-I-none ' Age, and it is very probable that the sacred vessels on that occasion were those commonly used by the humbler folk, perhaps a plate of earthenware and a cup of glass such as we have described.

SUMMARY

To sum up, one can only say that so far no relics of Christ or His Apostles have been discovered the authenticity of which can be established or even made to seem probable on purely archæological grounds. We possess, so far as can be proved, no utensil, tool, or any other article which was actually used by them as they went about their sacred business in the Holy Land of the early first century.

The New Testament itself contains no statement that such tangible mementoes were valued or preserved, although one can perhaps detect a hint or two of the beginnings of a sentiment which might very soon lead to the practice. There is, for example, the story of the people who brought handkerchieves and aprons from S. Paul's body to the bed-side of the sick (Acts xix, 12). But they, like the woman who touched the border of Christ's garment,

* R. Harris : *Glass Chalices of the First Century*, p. 9.

(S. Luke viii, 44), were hardly relic hunters. Not through souvenirs made by hand were we intended, it would seem, to keep alive the memory and preserve the spirit of the Founder of our Faith. *We look not at the things which are seen, but at the things which are not seen.* (II Corinthians iv, 18.)

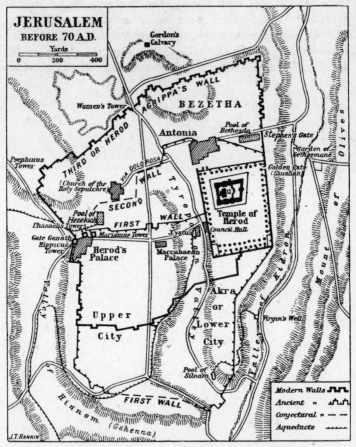

PLAN OF FIRST-CENTURY JERUSALEM
as reconstructed through the excavations.

III

JERUSALEM IN THE FIRST CENTURY

*Thus saith the Lord of hosts : Zion shall be plowed like a
field, and Jerusalem shall become heaps, and the
mountain of the house as the high places of a forest.*—
(Jeremiah xxvi. 18.)

THE search for possible relics of Christ and His Apostles
has lured us into by-paths somewhat remote from the
broad highway of archæology proper. We must now
examine the soil of Palestine itself, in case anything remains
above it or beneath which was actually in existence in the
first century of our era, and which may accordingly be
expected to illuminate the setting of the New Testament
scene. Though we may possess no relic of the things
which Jesus Himself actually handled, yet from another
point of view it may be even more enlightening to see with
our own eyes the things He saw with His, to walk in the
Master's footsteps along the roads He trod, and to steep
ourselves in the atmosphere of His life and times.

For such a quest there is more than merely sentimental
justification. By bringing His teaching into relation with its
environment, we shall surely understand it better : allusions
in the Gospel narrative, hitherto obscure, will now be
explained : in many ways a new sense of reality will be
given to the ' old, old story ' by making contact with the
tangible evidence for it which after all these twenty centuries
still survives.

As far as its physical features are concerned the Palestine
of to-day is naturally very much the same as it was in

New Testament times. The River Jordan must have looked the same to Jesus as it does to us, tumbling from the Lake of Galilee to the deep-set tropical basin of the Dead Sea. The hills are the same ; the same blue Mediterranean lashes the inhospitable coastline of what was once Philistia ; the climate cannot have altered much ; desert and stony wilderness still hang upon the fringe of garden and pasture land ; even the line of the ancient caravan tracks is probably still preserved by some of the modern highroads. Not all the macadam, concrete, railways, motor cars, up-to-date jerrybuilding, or barbed wire entanglements can ever quite destroy the unique character of the Holy Land, or prevent us from seeing it, on the whole, much as it appeared to Jesus Christ.*

DIFFICULTIES OF THE PROBLEM

As regards the antiquities of the land, however, we are on less certain ground.

On the one hand, we have the assistance of a peculiarly well-accredited tradition regarding the identification of the ancient sites. Interest in and memory for the past is notoriously retentive among Semitic peoples ; and of all Semites the Jews had a special incentive in their religion and in their love of the ancestral homeland to preserve an accurate recollection of bygone days. For centuries before the time of Christ, Palestine had been regarded as the ' Holy Land.' Pious Jews at home and pilgrims from abroad had long made a practice of venerating specially holy places connected with the revered characters and episodes of the Old Testament, and almost every ancient town or wayside landmark had some sacred association attached to it.

* For this aspect, read H. V. Morton's *In the Steps of the Master*, and G. A. Smith's *Historical Geography of the Holy Land*.

It is probable, therefore, that the earliest Christians (who were, for the most part, of Jewish stock) would remember certain spots and localities connected with their Master's earthly life. The scenes of His more notable actions or utterances would not easily be forgotten. It should be observed that the Gospels themselves, undoubted products of the first century, are careful to record the names of such places, almost as though the natural curiosity of future generations of pilgrims were being kept in view. So that the evidence of a long-established local tradition regarding the identification of the sacred sites should not be too lightly set aside.

On the other hand, one has to remember the great gulf that was made by certain historic events between the Palestine of the New Testament period and the Palestine of the second century. The ranks of the original Disciples, that is to say, those who had actually known Jesus in the flesh, were already thinning when, in the year A.D. 66, a vast conflagration raged over the Holy Land, obliterating in its passage many of the old familiar landmarks. The ruthless suppression of this Jewish Revolt and the total destruction of Jerusalem by Titus in A.D. 70 dropped an almost impenetrable curtain, archæologically speaking, between the earlier Jewish-Christian Church and the Gentile-Christian Church of later years. Amid the ruins of New Testament Jerusalem, a garrison consisting of the Tenth Legion (Fretensis) was left to complete the work of desolation, and for fifty years the Holy City disappeared from history.

Nor is that all. The siege of Titus was the *twentieth* suffered by Jerusalem, but it was not the last. After a while the indomitable city sprang Phœnix-like from its ashes, only to be demolished yet again, when Hadrian crushed the desperate rebellion of Bar Kochbar in A.D. 135. This time the exasperated Romans determined to expunge every trace of it. Planting a colony of soldiers in the ruins, they deliberately defiled the sacred sites, changed the name of the place to Aelia Capitolina, and forbade any Jew to visit it on pain of death, a prohibition which remained on the statute book for over two hundred years, though it is difficult to believe it was always strictly enforced.

There are thus two great gaps in the history of Christian Jerusalem*—a gap of fifty years after A.D. 70 and one of two centuries after A.D. 135.

How far, if at all, these gaps were bridged by the per-sistence of Christian tradition, is a difficult problem for the archæologist to solve. If the destruction of the city on either occasion was as thoroughgoing as the ancient his-torians assert, then it seems almost impossible that any genuine recollection of New Testament Jerusalem, still less any actual remains of it, could have survived. In other words, the popular ' tradition ' may have been a matter of pure imagination on the part of pious travellers of a far later date.

On the whole, however, the present-day tendency is to pay more regard than formerly to the traditional identifica-tion of the sacred sites, although, of course, not all tradition is of equal value. Much of it can be discarded at once, being obviously no more than mediæval or even modern Tourists' Tales. But some of it can be traced back as far as Constantine (about A.D. 330) or even earlier, and may have had its roots in an authentic recollection earlier still.

On behalf of this view, it is argued that the demolition of the city could never have been so complete as to conceal

---

* For the general history of Jerusalem, read C. A. Smith's *Jerusalem*.

all traces of its past ; that according to Hegesippus the
Jewish Christians who fled to Pella before the fall of
Jerusalem in A.D. 70 soon began creeping back to their
beloved Zion, and would surely never have allowed the
memory of the Holy Places to lapse ; that there was after
all an unbroken line of bishops of Jerusalem back to the
first century ; and that the Romans themselves in their
attempt to desecrate the Holy Places by building heathen
temples over them, thereby involuntarily preserved the sites
for ever. We shall recur to these points in more detail
as they arise.

THE CITY WALLS

*And the City lieth foursquare, and the length is as large as
the breadth.*—(Revelation xxi, 16.)

In following the discussion of the Holy Places the reader
may find it helpful to visualize the general plan of New
Testament Jerusalem as similar to a S. George's flag held
vertically. The outer walls enclose an area roughly square
in shape, which is divided again into four square spaces by a
central depression and a city wall running east and west,
and by the Tyropœon Valley running north and south. In
the north-east square lies the Temple and Bezetha. The
north-west square contains the Church of the Holy Sepulchre
and the ' Tower of David.' The south-east square includes
the Pool of Siloam, and the Akra, or Lower City. In the
south-west square is the Cœnaculum and the Protestant
Cemetery. The western side of the Tyropœon Valley is
known as the Upper City or (mistakenly) as the Hill of Zion.

It will be noticed by a comparison of the above rough
outline with a modern map of Jerusalem that the city walls
of Biblical times appear to have included less towards the

north and more towards the south than they do to-day. It must be our first task to trace the line of these walls as far as possible, and so to delimit the area of Herod's Jerusalem.

It is not as easy as it might appear at first sight, for, although the Jewish historian Josephus has left us a contemporary description of the walls, they were naturally the principal target of the Roman battering-rams in A.D. 70 and again in A.D. 135, and if there was one feature of the rebellious city which the conquerors on either occasion were more determined to annihilate than any other, it was the sturdy fortifications which had held them off so long. It has proved a matter of supreme difficulty, therefore, to trace the exact area of first-century Jerusalem, and the question is not finally settled even now.

THE FIRST WALL

The easiest wall to draw is the northern section of the Old, or what Josephus calls the ' First,' wall of the city, for here we are as certain as it is now possible to be of the two fixed points between which it ran in an almost straight line from west to east. According to the contemporary description,* this wall stretched from Herod's Castle, with its three great towers or keeps called Hippicus, Mariamne, and Phasæl on the west to a junction upon the west wall of the Temple. The site of the Temple is well established, as will be explained in our next chapter, and the junction of the First Wall with the Temple Wall, though not so far archæologically proved, must have been somewhere in the neighbourhood of Wilson's Arch, to the north of the colonnade called the Xystus and the Maccabæan Palace.

The site of Herod's Castle is located by general consent under the modern congeries of buildings known as *El-Kala*,

* Josephus : *Jewish War* V, 1 f.

or the Citadel, just south of the Jaffa Gate. Here the so-called ' Tower of David ' still stands as one of the few surviving monuments of Herod's long reign over Jerusalem. Restored in its present form during the fourteenth century, it preserves in the massive lower courses which rise steeply from the moated roadway, the actual stones built up by Herod over two thousand years ago. Apart from the minaret which surmounts it, the general appearance of the ' Tower of David ' to-day is probably not unlike the Phasæl of the first century ; an existing outwork, for instance, answers very closely to Josephus' description of a similar structure surrounding the keep in his day. The fortress was ninety cubits high, and furnished with battlements and turrets.

Of the sister Towers, Mariamne and Hippicus, probably only the foundations remain, but that the Citadel on the higher ground of this North-West Hill overlooking and dominating the Holy City below stands where the Castle of Herod once stood, cannot be doubted. Here, then, started the northern stretch of the Old Wall which finished at the Temple. In its course across the city it probably followed the contour of the natural depression running west and east, on a line just south of and parallel to the modern David Street and Temple Street. Some ancient foundations, possibly of wall courses, have in fact been discovered at the few places where excavation in this crowded quarter is possible.

Returning to Herod's Castle, we must now follow the line of wall which enclosed the southern part of the city. Here, where houses are fewer and a large area lies outside the modern wall, the difficulties of excavation are reduced, and much has been achieved in the search for actual remains of the ancient wall-courses. The names of Conder, Warren,

D

Bliss, Dickie, Guthe, Schick and Duncan are specially honoured in this connection.

From Phasæl and Mariamne, the Herodian wall struck almost due south, along the contour of the South-West Hill (now called ' Zion ') and Maudsley's Scarp to the present Protestant Cemetery. Here, at the south-west angle of the city, lay the ' Valley Gate ' mentioned in Nehemiah's well-known description of his tour of the walls (Nehemiah ii, 13), traces of which were discovered by Bliss.

From the Valley Gate the wall ran due east by the ' Dragon's Well ' (site unknown) along the southern edge of the South-West Hill for about 1,800 feet (several bastions on this line have been excavated) to the ' Dung Gate ' at the south-eastern angle of the city, where Bliss unearthed the remains of an ancient threshold.

From the Dung Gate the wall turned northwards over the Tyropœon Valley and in the direction of the Pool of Siloam, which, as the chief source of fresh water for the fortress of Zion, it must have enclosed. Running due north along the steep eastern slope of Ophel, the true site of David's Zion, it passed over the conduit from the Virgin's Spring (Gihon) and bent sharply eastward (at ' Guthe's Corner ') towards the ' Water Gate.' From this point it continued in a north-easterly line to Warren's ' Tower that standeth out ' until it joined the south-east angle of the Temple at the point where Warren discovered the remains of an ancient tower.

The rest of the Old Wall was identical in New Testament times with the outer wall of the Temple. At first it ran due north, overlooking the steep descent into the Kidron (Cedron) Valley. At that time, as we shall see, the Temple Wall did not extend as far north as it does to-day, but bending sharply north-west above the ' Golden Gate,' struck across (pierced only by the ' Sheep Gate ') to the Castle of Antonia, which protected it at a point where the natural defences were less secure. From Antonia the wall turned due south until it arrived at the junction near Wilson's Arch already mentioned.

We have thus completed the circuit of the Old or First Wall, and outlined the boundaries of Jerusalem as planned, in all probability, in the days of Solomon.

THE SECOND AND THIRD WALLS

In the first century A.D., however, the northern boundaries of the city included, as Josephus informs us, also a *Second* and a *Third* wall. For convenience and lucidity's sake it will be necessary to discuss these two together.

By the time of Hezekiah (*c.* 700 B.C.) houses had spread over the comparatively level ground to the north of the city, and a *Second* wall had been built beyond the Old Wall so as to enclose and protect the new suburb. This Second Wall, like the First, was restored by Nehemiah (*c.* 440 B.C.) and again by Herod the Great ; indeed, one would expect the latter to have paid especial attention to its reconstruction, for it guarded the only side of Jerusalem which was comparatively lacking in natural defences. It is described in some detail by Nehemiah (Nehemiah iii), and mentioned by Josephus. Nevertheless, it has been found impossible to define with any certainty even its approximate line.

All that we know from Josephus is that this Second Wall started at the Castle of Antonia, and made a junction with the Old Wall, at a Gate called Genath (the Garden Gate) somewhere near the Tower of Phasæl. Antonia we know, and Phasæl we know, but the Gate Genath has never been discovered. Nor have we any quite certain archæological evidence of the complicated line—it must have curved in and out—followed between those two points. (See below p. 43.) Nehemiah's description does not help us. The two towers he mentions, *Meah* and *Hananeel* (Nehemiah xii, 39), probably stood on the site of Antonia, so we may take them as a starting point. But the ' Fish Gate,' to which he next refers, is utterly unknown, and so are the other Gates, the ' Old Gate,' the ' Gate of Ephraim,' and so on, until he brings us to the ' Tower of the Furnaces,' which was probably near the Phasæl, where we were before.

The *Third* Wall described by Josephus is also a puzzle. It was not built until after the death of our Lord, but must have been well known (a section of it, at least) to S. Paul and the Apostles, its construction being started in A.D. 41 by Herod Agrippa I, King of the Jews. At the request of the Roman Emperor, building was soon discontinued, but the wall was hastily completed by the defenders of Jerusalem shortly before the final siege of A.D. 67. At the fall of the city in A.D. 70 it was, of course, completely destroyed.

Josephus tells us that this Third Wall started at the Tower of Hippicus (near Phasæl), extending northwards to the Tower of Psephinus. So far the line of this wall is not difficult to draw, for Psephinus can probably be located at the modern *Kasr Jalud* (Goliath's Castle), and traces of such a wall have been excavated. The rest of its course is not so easy. At Psephinus the wall turned eastward, ' marching down,' as Josephus puts it, ' right opposite the Monuments of Helena, Queen of Adiabene, where there was a Gate protected by the Women's Towers, continuing through the Royal Caverns, and turning at the Fuller's Monument to join the older wall above the Kidron Valley. It thus enclosed the suburb of Bezetha north of the Temple.' Unfortunately, with the exception of the large area known as Bezetha, none of the above-named landmarks has been identified with certainty.

It will make the matter clearer if we now state separately the two conflicting theories as to the actual course followed by these Second and Third Walls.

A. The first, which we call the traditional theory upheld by Wilson, George Adam Smith,* and the majority, perhaps, of modern archæologists, is as follows : The Second Wall must have run from a point upon the Old Wall near the ' Tower of David ' in a north-easterly direction, curving so as to leave the Church of the Holy Sepulchre outside it, and bending east again above the Via Dolorosa till it joined the Castle of Antonia and so completed the circuit. It is admitted that no *certain* archæological proof of this line has been discovered, but on the other hand little real excavation has been possible, owing to the crowded buildings on the area. Merrill and Schick, however, believed that they had found traces of this Second Wall at various points. Also the Russian excavations east of the Church revealed some interesting remains. An archway with two supporting columns is a relic of Constantine's Atrium approaching the Holy Places. There is also a massive wall-angle of apparently Herodian or earlier construction in proximity to an ancient door lintel, fitted for revolving gates, which has been claimed as the site of the Judgement Gate in the city wall through which Christ passed to His death.

It will be noticed that the Church of the Holy Sepulchre, claiming to cover the site of Calvary, is thus left ' *outside* the city wall,' an essential condition if the identification is to square with the Scriptures (Hebrews xiii, 12).

On this theory, the Third Wall mentioned by Josephus must have followed the course of the modern north wall,

* C. W. Wilson : *Golgotha and the Holy Sepulchre.* G. A. Smith : *Jerusalem.*

running from the Citadel (Hippicus) to Goliath's Castle
(Psephinus), thence across to the Damascus Gate. To the
north of this gate lie the so-called ' Tombs of the Kings,'
or ' Tombs of the Sultans,' where the Monuments of
Queen Helena have been located, thus establishing another
link with Josephus'.description ; and on this theory the
' Women's Towers ' must have been somewhere near.
From the Damascus Gate the wall stretched, as it stretches
now, over the ' Cotton Grotto ' (the Royal Caverns) to
' Herod's Gate,' and so to ' Stork's Tower,' where it bent
sharply south to ' S. Stephen's Gate,' thus enclosing Bezetha
and the Birket Israin (Israel). That there did actually exist
an ancient fortified wall along this line has been proved by
excavation, and the presence of houses within this area in
New Testament times may be taken as established.

The fact that on this theory the traditional site of the
Holy Sepulchre lies *within* one of the city walls does not
affect the question, because this particular wall was not
built until after the Crucifixion.

B. We must now consider the other, or what we may
call Robinson's, theory* about the two walls, which had
the general support of Fergusson, Merrill, Conder, and
others. This theory depends on the awkward fact that
the famous American investigator, Dr. Robinson, a hundred
years ago, discovered the remains of what he believed to
be a first-century wall running on a line parallel with, but
over a quarter of a mile to the north of, the modern city
wall. If this was not the Third Wall, what wall could it
have been ?—for there is no record of a fourth. Robinson
accordingly drew the line of the Third (Agrippa's) Wall
from the Citadel (Hippicus) to the modern Russian Cathedral
(400 yards north of Goliath's Castle), where he located the

---

* E. Robinson : *Biblical Researches in Palestine* (1841).

site of Psephinus. Thence, he thought, the wall ran straight to a point midway between the ' Tombs of the Kings ' and the ' Grotto of Jeremiah,' thus coming close to the supposed Monuments of Helena on the former site, and eventually enclosing Bezetha, as Josephus states.

On this theory, of course, the modern city wall must have been the true *Second* Wall ; and the *traditional* ' Second Wall ' running south of the Holy Sepulchre never existed at all, except in the imagination of the traditionalists. Calvary, Golgotha, and the Sepulchre of Jesus, therefore, could not possibly have been where Constantine supposed, and a location somewhere outside the modern wall must be sought. Such a location has, in fact, been suggested, as we shall explain in our remarks on ' Gordon's Calvary.'

Robinson's discovery of supposedly ancient wall-courses so far to the north has, however, been severely questioned. The stones he unearthed seem to have been quickly removed by local builders, and are not there to-day. The Ordnance Survey of 1865 declared that the remains of ' Robinson's Wall ' ' could not have formed part of a wall of defence,' and in any case they are nowhere near the ' Royal Caverns ' through which Josephus said the Third Wall ran. Moreover, it is almost inconceivable that first-century Jerusalem could have covered so large an area to the north of the modern city and no traces have been found here of extensive habitation. Accordingly, in spite of Mayer and Sukenik's discovery of further masonry along Robinson's line in 1925,* this theory of the walls has been generally abandoned, and the traditional identification prevails.

* L. A. Mayer and E. L. Sukenik : *The Third Wall of Jerusalem* (1930).

Having settled, as far as possible, the boundaries of Herod's Jerusalem, we must now enquire if any first-century remains or sites can still be identified within the city. We know something of his celebrated Temple, as will be seen, but where lay the Palace of the Hasmoneans (Maccabees) which Herod's wife Mariamne gave him as her dowry, and where must we seek the lovely marble colonnade called the Xystos, or the magnificent Greek Hippodrome which caused such scandal to the orthodox ?

Alas, not one stone remains upon another which can be shown beyond doubt to have belonged to these once splendid edifices.

All that is left as a tangible memento of Herod's architecture, apart from what has already been mentioned, such as the walls and the ' Tower of David,' are some ashlar walling and Corinthian column bases near the Church of the Holy Sepulchre. These are probably the remains of a King's Highway, or *Via Principalis*, built for the use of state processions entering the city from the north.

As so often, if we wish to reconstruct in our mind's eye the appearance of Herod's Jerusalem at the height of its glory, we must turn to ruins elsewhere in Palestine and better preserved. The best example, for instance, of a Herodian *Via Principalis* is to be seen in Jerash (Gerasa), where the whole of the town plan is still clearly visible. Rows of broken columns and Corinthian pillars, 230 in all, mark the main street, while side-streets intersect it at regular intervals, the junction being marked by marble colonnades and decorated archways. Other ruins on this site—a triumphal arch, splendid baths, a theatre seating six thousand spectators, the portico of a lofty temple, and so on—indicate the type of architecture in which this Hellenizing monarch took pride.   There are also the ruins of an interesting synagogue, with a colonnaded entrance, a mosaic of the Flood depicting the procession of animals entering the Ark, and an inscription in Hebrew : *Amen. Selah: peace to the synagogue* (*c.* A.D. 400).

There are similar remains at various other sites up and down the country.   At Amman still survive the striking ruins of a magnificent Græco-Roman amphitheatre, cut by Ptolemy Philadelphus out of the hillside, its tiers of rock-hewn seats separated by terraces, with the remains of a stately colonnaded entrance and royal box.   Frank Mountain, a few miles south of Jerusalem, preserves a few remains of Herod's Castle, with its four round towers, where the tyrant was buried.   Near Banias (Cæsarea Philippi) is a grotto carved out of the living rock by Herod himself, in honour of the Emperor Augustus, as a shrine to the pagan nature-god Pan—a curious sidelight on the extremely liberal theology of the man who built the Temple of Jehovah in Jerusalem !   There is also a massive fortress here, the portal of which may date from the days of Philip, Tetrarch of Galilee (Herod's son), who rebuilt the town. At Makaur (Machærus), where John the Baptist was beheaded, the ruins of the fortress rebuilt by Herod may still be seen.   Sebastiyeh (Samaria) is a veritable storehouse of antiques and ancient ruins.   Here the ivory palace of Ahab has been excavated, and many Herodian remains, such as a well-preserved Roman altar, a colossal statue of Augustus, and the foundations of a huge temple erected in honour of the same emperor, together with two magnificent flights of steps seventy feet wide.   A Roman gateway flanked by two round towers has also been discovered here, and a noble *Via Principalis* a mile long, lined with columns sixteen

feet in height.   At Tell-Sandahannah (Saint Anna) almost
an entire Jewish-Greek town of the first century has been
laid bare, with its walls, gates, streets, and private houses,
together with a statuette of Astarte which looks remarkably
like a model of Saint Anne herself, complete with halo and
flowing robes.

The Græco-Roman remains as a whole thus enable us to
conjecture with some sort of certainty the type of architecture and art in general which must have prevailed in
the Jerusalem of New Testament days.   They remind us
that Judæa at that period was just as thickly covered with
the outward and visible signs of Hellenistic culture as any
other province of the Empire, however little one would
have suspected it from a reading of the Gospel narrative.
The Jewish writers had a strange power of ignoring what
they disliked !

THE CITY ENVIRONS

*Walk about Sion, and go round about her : and tell the
towers thereof.   Mark well her bulwarks.*—(Psalm xlviii, 11.)

We will now leave the city itself and examine its immediate outskirts.

A very striking group of monuments is that which faces
towards the Temple from the opposite side of the Kidron
Valley on the east.   It comprises (1) the so-called *Tomb
of Absalom*, a square mausoleum with an Ionic façade,
surmounted by a cupola in the shape of an inverted tundish
or funnel ; (2) the *Grotto of S. James*, with windows and
a Doric portico ; (3) the *Pyramid of Zacharias*, carved in
the form of a fluted cube upon which stands a pyramid-like
roof.   All three are carved out of the living rock in a mixture

of the Greek and Egyptian styles. These quaint monuments
date undoubtedly from the first century or earlier, and
must have been familiar objects to our Lord as He went
towards the Mount of Olives.

They are all—as is so often the case in Palestine—quite
fantastically misnamed. (1) The ' Tomb of Absalom,'
sometimes called ' Pharaoh's Pillar,' is probably the
mausoleum of Alexander Jannæus, one of the Maccabæan
governors of Jerusalem, made in 78 B.C. (2) The ' Grotto
of S. James ' has an important inscription in square Hebrew
characters (one of the earliest examples of this script) showing it to have been the burial place of the Sons of Hezir mentioned in I Chronicles xxiv, 15. The inscription reads :
*This tomb and . . . to Eleazar, Haniah, Joazar, Jehudah,
Simon, Johanan son of Joseph son . . . Joseph and Eleazar,
sons of Haniah . . . of the Sons of Hezir.* The tomb was
probably built about 10 B.C. Its inner chamber was completely excavated by Ganneau, who found two arcades
erected over slabs on which sarcophagi (stone coffins) were
placed. It had evidently been used at one time as a place
of residence ! (3) Of the ' Tomb of Zacharias ' nothing
seems to be known.

To the south-west of these monuments, and close to the
slope of Ophel, is the *Virgin's Spring*. In this case the
name is better chosen, for it is the only fountain of drinking
water on this side of Jerusalem, and the Blessed Virgin,
during her stay in the City,* may well have been accustomed
to descend from the water-gate with a pitcher under her
arm to draw at this well. It is identical, most probably, with
the Gihon or En Rogel of the Old Testament.

From this fountain runs the famous subterranean *Siloam
Tunnel* excavated by Hezekiah in 701 B.C. when expecting

* Tradition has it that she was born and died in Jerusalem.

blockade by the Assyrians.* The tunnel carries water from the Virgin's Spring to a steep-sided reservoir (the *Ain Silwan*) within the ancient walls, so that a beleaguered garrison should not go short of supplies. This reservoir is probably the ancient Pool of Siloam, whose waters were believed to have healing properties (S. John ix, 7).† A curious spasmodic action of the fountain bubbling from the well of Gihon causes a sudden ebb and flow of the waters in the pool, so that one is tempted to identify it with the Pool of Bethesda, also mentioned in S. John's Gospel (S. John v, 2), although it is nowhere near any known ' Sheep Market.' Another suggested identification of the Pool of Bethesda is the Birket Israin just north of the Temple, which suits the geographical notices better, but on the other hand it does not exhibit anything like a ' troubling of the waters.' This is one of the cruxes of New Testament archæology.

On the northern side of the city, just within the modern wall near to the Damascus Gate, lies the ' Cotton Grotto,' otherwise called the *Royal Caverns*. It is an extensive subterranean quarry stretching over two hundred yards to the south. Niches for the quarrymen's lamps are still visible in the rocky sides, as well as marks of the wooden wedges by which the stones were removed. The *Grotto of Jeremiah*, just outside the wall, is a similar underground quarry, originally a continuation of the above. Here, as we shall see, lies the celebrated ' Garden Tomb.'

Farther to the north are the *Tombs of the Kings* (Tombs of the Sultans), where one descends a stone stairway into a vaulted underground chamber, decorated with ornamental carvings. Within it are some sarcophagi and tomb-spaces,

---

* S. L. Caiger : *Bible and Spade*, p. 154 f.

† To the south of this pool lies the so-called Lower Pool of Siloam (the *Birket el-Hamra*) which was probably the ' King's Pool ' of Nehemiah ii, 14. It is connected by an ancient aqueduct with the Virgin's Fount.

some of them in separate cavities of their own—it is a kind of Jewish catacomb, in fact. Here, in the opinion of many experts, were the *Monuments of Helena* mentioned by Josephus as a landmark on the north of Jerusalem. Helena, Queen of Adiabene, was a contemporary of S. Paul. She had been converted to Judaism, and sent corn to Jerusalem at the time of the famine mentioned in Acts xi, 28. She is stated to have built her family tomb half a mile outside the city, and to have been buried here on her death. De Saulcy found on one of the sarcophagi an Aramaic inscription with the name of *Sarah*, which he believed to be Queen Helena's Jewish name. The body, however, crumbled to dust when the lid was raised. Somewhere near these ' Tombs of the Kings,' therefore, if this identification is correct, the three conspicuous Pyramids mentioned by Josephus must have stood, and it is said that parts of their foundations still remain.

But the location of Helena's Pyramids on this spot does not quite tally with the measurements and other indications given by Josephus, and good reason has been shown for placing them considerably farther to the south-west on the Nablus road.* In this position, being in the direct line of march of the Roman armies at the siege of A.D. 70, they must inevitably have been destroyed.

Of Pontius Pilate, one unquestionably authentic relic survives. On the road from Jerusalem to Bethlehem, half-buried in the ground, lie the remains of an aqueduct which the Roman governor is recorded to have constructed from Solomon's Pool to the Temple area. One can still see those huge blocks of rounded stone drilled with a central hole and flanged so as to fit into one other, which are the sole remaining monument of Pilate's rule over the Holy City.

* N. P. Clarke in *P.E.F.Q.*, April, 1938.

IV

JERUSALEM AND THE HOLY PLACES

*O God, the heathen are come into Thine inheritance : Thy
holy Temple have they defiled, and made Jerusalem an
heap of stones.*—(Psalm lxxix, 1.)

MANY ' Holy Places ' are pointed out to the tourist in
Jerusalem by the voluble Arab guide who is ever ready
to supply the demands of credulity in proportion to
baksheesh offered. Here in the Church of the Holy
Sepulchre is shown an actual Footprint of Christ ; this
depression in a stone on the Via Dolorosa was caused by His
straining Hand as He drooped under the weight of the
Cross ; there stands the house of S. Veronica, who wiped
His Face with her handkerchief, and so on. But such
marvels, however helpful to devotion, fall not within our
present scope. ' No confidence,' as the Guide Book* drily
observes, ' should be placed in the explanation of the
antiquities given by these street-guides or by the dragomans
proper,' so we shall not, as a rule, repeat them.

A few of these popular traditions, however, have a certain
claim on our attention, if only because of their long association with Christian piety in the past. Even if the time-
honoured identification turn out to be wholly incorrect, a
place which has been venerated for centuries as enshrining
some memory of the earthly life of Jesus has become, as it
were, holy in its own right.

* Baedeker's *Syria and Palestine.*

GOLGOTHA AND THE HOLY SEPULCHRE

Wherefore Jesus also, that He might sanctify the people with His own blood, suffered without the gate. Let us go forth therefore unto Him without the camp, bearing His reproach.—(Hebrews xiii, 12, 13.)

Whatever may be thought, for instance, about its archæological credentials, no one can surely look unmoved upon the ancient Church of the Holy Sepulchre, where for over sixteen hundred years Christians of all nations have knelt and wept upon the actual site, as they believe, of the Saviour's Crucifixion, Burial, and Resurrection from the dead.

Entering to-day this sacred shrine built on the very spot where Constantine dedicated his celebrated Basilica in A.D. 336, one needs but little imagination to feel again something of that emotion which has stirred so many ages of pilgrims to prayer and praise. We are walking now, if not in the very footprints of the Master, at least in the steps of countless generations of His saints. This is the Holy Place of which the pilgrim Sophronius* wrote over thirteen centuries ago (A.D. 610), dreaming that one day through the goodness of God he might be allowed to see it :—

O thou holy City of God, Jerusalem, would that I were now within thy gates !   Then would I draw near to the Church of the Holy Sepulchre, from whence the Lord of all rose again from the dead.   I would kiss the earth, the sweet earth, feast my eyes upon the sacred dome, and the lofty rotunda with its four apses.   Crossing the splendid chancel, I would come to the Sepulchre of Jesus in the midst thereof, kissing with deep devotion the stone whereon He was laid, and dancing with joy as I embraced the columns round about it, with their capitals of

* Quoted in G. Dalman's *Sacred Sites and Ways.*

*golden lilies !   Then I would draw near to the Place of the
Skull, and would lie at full length and kiss that stone which is
the sacred centre of the world.*

From the time of Constantine till now, an unending
stream of pilgrims to the Holy Land has made the Church
of the Holy Sepulchre its holiest shrine, and to hundreds of
thousands of Christians it is still ' the sacred centre of the
world.'   The most celebrated of all religious ceremonies in
Jerusalem are to this day the Easter Rites and Exposition of
the Holy Fire in this ancient church—though temporarily
discontinued in 1938 by order of the British Government,
owing to an earthquake having rendered the building unsafe.

It is not with the Church of the Holy Sepulchre, however,
architecturally interesting though it may be, but with the site
upon which it stands that we are now concerned.   What
archæological evidence is there, if any, to prove that tradition
is correct in its identification of this site with Calvary and the
Tomb where the Body of Jesus was laid ?

We need spend little time in showing that the site of the
present church (built by the Crusaders in 1099) is virtually
identical with that of the fourth-century basilica erected by
the Emperor Constantine.   An unbroken literary tradition
asserts that it is so ; the remains of a Roman portico or
atrium may still be seen ; and we have the evidence of the
fifth-century Madeba Map which shows the Church of the
Holy Sepulchre in precisely its present position.

This celebrated map of Palestine and the Near East was
constructed in variegated mosaic on the floor of a Byzantine
church in the little village of Madeba near Heshbon.   It had
been covered up by a pavement, but was cleared in 1896 and
partially restored (Plate III).   It is fortunate that the best
preserved portion of the mosaic is the section showing
Jerusalem.   It is of exquisite execution in the usual antique

Plate III

THE OLDEST MAP OF JERUSALEM
The Madeba Mosaic
(*See page* 54)

THE GARDEN TOMB
Was Jesus buried here?
(*See page* 58)

cartographist's style, yet strikingly anticipating in its method of coloration our modern physiographical maps—plains are tinted light brown, mountains a darker brown, and the sea a deep green. The locations of many New Testament sites are shown with such minute care that even the buildings in Jerusalem can be distinguished, while a pennon in Greek characters attached to each locality indicates its name. The date at which it was made is believed to be the fifth or early sixth century. The Madeba Map, therefore, has proved invaluable in the identification ·of Biblical sites as accepted by the Church in very early tradition ; though useless, of course, for proving the *authenticity* of such tradition.

Taking it as proved, then, that the present Church is on the site selected by Constantine, we must now examine his reasons for choosing it. Here we are fortunate in having an almost contemporary account of the episode in the works of the historian Eusebius.* He tells us that shortly after the Council of Nicæa (A.D. 325) Constantine determined to consecrate the exact site of the Resurrection and to mark it for Christians of all time by building over it a memorial Church. There seems to have been no question as to the precise locality of the Resurrection, for Hadrian in A.D. 135 was said to have built thereon a Temple of Venus (Aphrodite) with the express purpose of defiling it. All that Constantine had to do was to clear away this Pagan Temple, and substitute a Christian Church. So far Eusebius.

This is good contemporary evidence that the present-day tradition goes back at all events to Constantine. And if Hadrian really did build that Temple of Venus with the purpose ascribed to him (which, though unproven, is not at all unlikely), then the tradition goes back two centuries earlier still. But now comes that gap of which we have

---

* Eusebius : *Life of Constantine* iii, 25ff.

already spoken, the fifty-year gap between A.D. 70, when Jerusalem ceased to exist and about A.D. 120, when the city began to rise again. Supposing there was a tradition about the site of the Holy Sepulchre in A.D. 120 (namely, the tradition which Hadrian believed), was it a genuine recollection passed on from nearly a century earlier (the Crucifixion took place in A.D. 29), or was it a pious improvization of the second-century Church ?

Archæology can offer no demonstrative proof, one way or another, but certain circumstantial evidence has emerged which, in the opinion of many, goes far to corroborate Constantine's (and Hadrian's) choice of site. While clearing away the Temple of Venus in order to lay the foundations of the new Church in A.D. 330, Bishop Macarius, we are told, suddenly came upon an ancient rock-tomb cut deep below the surface. Although believing that this was the true site of the Burial, he had not expected, after the lapse of three centuries, to find that the actual Sepulchre of our Lord had survived (see p. 10). But the position of this newly-discovered tomb, as well as its conformity to the indications given in the Gospel narrative, made it inevitable that it should be hailed at once as the Holy Sepulchre itself. And from that day to this it has been so revered, though altered almost beyond recognition in the interests of architecture and devotion.

The Holy Sepulchre to-day is a small cell, six and a half feet long and six feet wide, the original rock-face of the interior being covered with marble. From the ceiling hang forty-three lamps, illuminating a relief in white marble showing Christ rising from the dead. On one side is a shelf of solid stone, five feet long, two feet wide, and a yard high, also covered with marble—the stone where the body of Jesus lay, and on which Peter and John saw the linen clothes lying, that first Easter morning (S. John xx, 5). The Sepulchre is entered by a low door from which it is possible to look down into the interior. Nearby is a stone set in marble, said to be the stone which covered the entrance to the Tomb. There is no trace, of course, of the Garden of Joseph of Arimathea, nor of the city wall outside which the place of burial lay, but there is nothing archæologically impossible in the situation of the Tomb itself.

Not far away—it should be understood that all the Holy Places connected immediately with the Crucifixion and the Resurrection are now enclosed under one roof—is a flight of stone steps leading down to the Cavern of the Invention of the Cross, where Constantine is said to have found the True Wood (see page 10f). An adjacent stone stairway leads up to the Hill of Golgotha, or Mount Calvary, the ' Place of a Skull,' upon which the Crucifixion itself is believed to have taken place. Here are shown the exact spots where the three crosses were fixed in the ground—far too close together, one would say. The rock-surface of the mound is not visible now, as it is overbuilt by the church walls, but about five feet away from the Cross of Christ is the famous Rent in the Rock (S. Matthew xxvii, 51), through which a glimpse of the original cliff may be seen, and which is said to reach to the centre of the earth !

To this brief description of the most sacred site in Christendom, nothing much of archæological importance can be added. The site itself is a possible one, though a great deal depends, as we have seen, upon our delineation of the course of the Second Wall. If this ' Second Wall ' followed the line of the modern city wall, as Robinson and others believed, then the Church of the Holy Sepulchre lay *within* the ancient city, and therefore cannot mark the true site of Golgotha. If, on the other hand, the Second Wall ran to the south and east of Constantine's Church, then the traditional site may well be genuine.

GORDON'S CALVARY AND THE GARDEN TOMB

And when they were come unto a place called Golgotha, that is to say, a place of a skull.—(S. Matthew xxvii, 33.)

For those who reject the traditional identification, the site now called ' Gordon's Calvary ' or the ' Protestant Calvary ' still provides a satisfying alternative. It is to the north of Jerusalem, and well outside all possible city walls —a great rugged cliff of limestone facing the Damascus Gate. Here General Gordon made up his mind that the true site of Calvary must be sought.

The attraction of this cliff, as a possible site of the Crucifixion, is felt at the very first view of it, for the eye-sockets, nose and mouth of a human countenance are clearly perceived upon the fissured and weather-worn surface of the rock, and might well, one admits, have caused it to be known as the Place of a Skull.' It is only on second thoughts that one asks, Were those skull-like holes and marks really in existence two thousand years ago, or are they the result of later quarrying, wear, and tear ? And was Golgotha so named after the physical appearance of the place, or after the ancient tradition that on it the Skull of Adam had been found ?

Again, however, the site is not impossible. It lay in full view of the city walls, and at such a road-junction (of the Nablus and Jericho roads) as the Romans often chose for their executions for the sake of publicity. A respectable Jewish tradition, too, still persists that here was the regular place for stoning offenders against the Law—such as S. Stephen. If this is the case—that S. Stephen was stoned on the site of the Crucifixion—it would lend additional poignancy to the Martyr's dying prayer : ' Lord, lay not this sin to their charge ! ' (Acts vii, 60), as though he were recalling his Master's cry, ' Father, forgive them ; for they know not what they do ! ' (S. Luke xxiii, 34). But one would expect so striking a coincidence of locality to have been noted in the text.

This site, at any rate—first proposed by Otto Thenius in 1842—has been upheld against the traditional view by several well-known writers on the topography of ancient Jerusalem, such as Conder, Merrill, Renan, Rider Haggard, Hanauer, Macmillan's Guide to Palestine, and, best known of all, General Gordon of Khartoum, after whom it is now usually named.

If ' Gordon's Calvary ' is really the true site of the Crucifixion, then the so-called ' Garden Tomb ' (Plate III) may well be the true Holy Sepulchre, for there is no other ancient tomb in the vicinity that so well satisfies the Scriptural narrative. Conder indeed proposed another tomb, but it is nearly two hundred yards distant, and is now forgotten, while the Garden Tomb (often erroneously known as ' Gordon's Tomb ') has grown in favour.

This tomb, accidentally discovered in 1867, consists of a sunken chamber excavated in the rock, to which access is given by a small oblong door. In front of the door is a kind of channel or groove, which in Crusaders' days was used as a trough for horses, but may originally have been intended to serve as a runner for a large stone which could be rolled over the entrance. The chamber within the tomb holds three recesses, each intended to enclose a stone shelf or platform upon which a body could rest. But in only one of these is the carving completely finished. From the doorway it is possible to look inside and see one of the shelves, the completed one. The tomb thus answers the Scriptural description—it was ' a sepulchre that was hewn in stone, wherein never man before was laid ' (S. Luke xxiii, 53) ; it was possible for S. John ' stooping down and looking in, to see the linen clothes lying.' (S. John xx, 5) ; and the entrance was probably closed by a stone (S. Luke xxiv, 2).

Many archæologists agree with Schick that this tomb is of characteristically Jewish construction, and quite possibly of early first-century date, although the presence of ecclesiastical emblems and other indications show that it was used for Christian burials in the fourth century.

A thorough excavation of the tomb in 1923 (by Miss Hussey) disclosed, at a depth of eighteen feet, a remarkable stone carving shaped like a shrine of Venus, including the customary pigeon-holes and the sacred tree of Adonis. This has been claimed as a relic of the Temple of Venus which Hadrian built over the site of the Crucifixion, and as evidence therefore for the genuineness of the Garden Tomb.* In that case, of course, it has to be assumed that Constantine mistook the true site of Hadrian's temple when he built his basilica.

THE VIA DOLOROSA

When Pilate therefore heard that saying, he brought Jesus forth, and sat down in the judgment seat in a place that is called The Pavement, but in the Hebrew, Gabbatha.— (S. John xix, 13.)

By the ' Via Dolorosa,' or ' Way of Sorrows,' is meant the route which our Lord followed from the Judgment Hall of Pilate (the Prætorium) to the city gate and thence

---

* Bent and Hussey : *Golgotha and the Garden Tomb.*

to the Place of Crucifixion outside the walls. To-day the line of this route is drawn from the Ecce Homo (' Behold the Man ') Arch along the Via Dolorosa Street to the Church of the Holy Sepulchre, and is marked by fourteen ' Stations of the Cross ' commemorating various incidents in the journey.

The Via Dolorosa can hardly, of course, preserve the *exact* route of the Crucifixion procession, for the streets through which Jesus passed had been entirely obliterated more than once before the ' Stations of the Cross ' were invented by Franciscan friars in the fourteenth century. Whether it preserves the true *general* direction of our Lord's last journey must depend upon oui view of the site not only of Golgotha but of Pilate's Prætorium, or ' Judgment-seat.' The problem of Golgotha has already been discussed. It remains to consider the identification of the Prætorium.

The traditional view locates the Judgment Hall, where the last Trial of Jesus took place, at the Castle of Antonia, north-west of the Temple, where the Ecce Homo Arch, now partly blocked by an altar with the inscription ' Father, forgive them, for they know not what they do ' (in Latin), commemorates Pilate's last appeal to the compassion of the mob. The Arch itself is admittedly of second-century (Hadrian's) construction, but recent excavations (by Vincent) have shown that it stands on a first-century pavement (the ' Gabbatha ' of the Gospel ?) which formed the central court of Herod's Castle of Antonia. So that the Ecce Homo Arch may be more correctly named than has usually been supposed (see p. 71).

Some, however, contend that the Prætorium in Jerusalem (that is to say, the Headquarters of the Roman Governor) could not have been anywhere else than in the great fortress of Herod's Palace on the north-west hill (the present

' Tower of David ') which Pontius Pilate is known to have taken over as his official residence. Here, according to this view, must ' Gabbatha,' the Governor's public ' Pavement ' or platform, be located—where Allenby in fact caused his proclamation of the capture of Jerusalem to be read to the populace in 1917—and from here, it is said, the Way of Sorrows must have begun.

But again it is argued that the Prætorium was not necessarily identical with the Governor's residence. It could be set up at any spot where he happened to be exercising his judicial office, and at such a time of tension as the Jewish Passover, it may well have been that Pilate took up a strategic position at the celebrated Castle of Antonia, erected by Herod the Great to overawe and dominate the seat of most of the trouble in Jerusalem, the Temple. The tradition, therefore, that our Lord's last Trial and the beginning of His Via Dolorosa is to be sought on the site of the Ecce Homo Arch may be historically correct.

THE UPPER ROOM

Ye shall say unto the goodman of the house, The Master saith unto thee, Where is the guestchamber, where I shall eat the Passover with My Disciples? And he shall shew you a large upper room furnished : there make ready. (S. Luke xxii, 11, 12.)

One other Holy Place in Jerusalem must be noticed. In the south-west area of the city lies a large congeries of buildings known as the ' Tomb of the Prophet David.' Here are subterranean chambers revered by the Mohammedans as containing the sarcophagus of King David, while on the first floor above is a room no less revered by

Christians as the traditional Upper Room where the Last Supper was held, and where the Holy Spirit descended on the Church at Pentecost. A stone seat is pointed out as our Lord's, and the place of the Holy Table is shown.

This room, usually known as the Cœnaculum or Cenacle (Supper Room), is of fourteenth century Franciscan construction, but was built on an original site of much earlier date—part of the eastern wall is apparently Byzantine. The tradition has a somewhat complicated pedigree, traceable as far back as the fourth century, but in its earliest form relating only to the Upper Room of Pentecost, which was said to have been one of the very few houses to survive the destruction of Jerusalem by the Romans. The Upper Room of Pentecost, however, was not at first identified with the Upper Room of the Eucharist, nor was it until the fifth century that the Maundy Thursday anniversary Communion was here celebrated, so that the archæological and historical evidence for the authenticity of the Cœnaculum is slender. Incidentally, the tradition that David was buried here, rather than within his own city on the Hill of Ophel (cf. Nehemiah iii, 16), is still more improbable. David's Tomb was still well known at the time of the New Testament (Acts ii, 29) and is described by Josephus. According to Conder ' this description applies only to one known ancient tomb in Jerusalem, namely the so-called Tomb of Joseph of Arimathea and Nicodemus,' near the Holy Sepulchre, a suggested identification accepted by few.

Equally slender is the evidence for most of the other Holy Places shown to the pilgrim. In the nature of the case their authenticity cannot be proved. Nor, from the spiritual or doctrinal point of view, is it very necessary. Of one thing, after all, we can be quite certain : that somewhere within a stone's throw of the sites commonly pointed out, our Lord did indeed eat His last supper, tread the weary Way of Sorrows, and suffer death upon the Cross.

THE TEMPLE

His disciples came to Him for to shew Him the buildings of the Temple. And Jesus said unto them, See ye not all these things? Verily I say unto you, There shall not be left one stone upon another, that shall not be thrown down.—(S. Matthew xxiv, 1, 2.)

The Temple of Herod the Great (sometimes called the Third Temple) in which our Lord and His Apostles worshipped, must have been one of the most imposing sacred edifices not only in Palestine, but in the world. According to contemporary descriptions, in extent it exceeded the famous Altis of Olympia and the Acropolis of Athens. The Porch had a colonnade seven hundred feet long. Eighteen marble pillars, one hundred feet high, supported the central aisle, which was thus higher and longer than York Minster. One of the nine gates which gave entrance to it was so heavy that twenty men were needed to open and close it. And the whole building, constructed of limestone so white that it shone like ivory, except where the façade of the Inner Court was inlaid with gleaming gold, towered magnificently within its spacious enclosure over the Kidron Valley and proclaimed afar the Glory of the Lord of Hosts.

One of the tragedies of Jewish history is that the finishing touches had scarcely been added to this splendid shrine before the Roman soldiery brought it tumbling to the ground, with as much indifference to its supreme beauty as though it had been a mud hovel. Thus from A.D. 70 to the present day scarcely a trace of its former splendour survives to help us visualize the Temple as it was in the days of our Lord.

Its site, however, is one of the few in Jerusalem of which we can be virtually certain. Only dynamite could destroy the natural features of the rock on which it was built, and even Titus' mighty siege-engines could not entirely smash the massive masonry of its foundations. Moreover, the very eagerness of the Roman to obliterate the shrine which had inspired such fanatical uprisings, served only to preserve its identity. To-day an ancient Mohammedan Mosque, the Haram esh-Sheriff, stands guard over the exact spot where three thousand years ago King David chose a site for the Altar of his God by the Threshing-floor of Araunah the Jebusite, where Solomon built his House of the Lord ' exceedingly magnifical,' where Zerubbabel restored it after its destruction, and where Herod the Great erected at last the grandest and most beautiful Temple of all.

The position of the ancient Altar of Sacrifice, indeed the actual base of that Altar, can still be seen exactly as it was from time immemorial and unto the days of our Lord. Under the Dome of the Rock (*Es-Sakhra*), sometimes called the Mosque of Omar, is a square enclosure about sixty feet long by forty-five feet wide, within which lies a great, rugged platform of natural rock, an outcrop from the foundations beneath the building (Plate IV). Rising to five or six feet above the level of the floor, this strange platform carries us back to the very beginnings of sacrifice in Canaan, its primeval crudity all the more striking by contrast with the elaborate artistry of the surrounding Moslem shrine. The channel which conveyed the blood of the sacrifice to an underground chamber is still clearly seen, and in its vicinity still remain the cisterns which held the water wherewith it was washed by the Priests and Levites of old.

Systematic excavation of so sacred a place as the Haram has naturally been prohibited, but occasionally chance subsidences or necessary structural repairs have enabled the European archæologist to explore. Underneath the ground, the Temple area seems to consist of a veritable maze of caverns, vaults, and secret passages. Captain Warren, one of the earliest explorers (1865), found no less than thirty-three underground cisterns and a plentiful supply of flowing water. Many of the subterranean vaults are artificially built up of strong arches supporting the soil overhead, with the object, apparently, of securing a level surface for the Temple Court which is now partially covered by the Mosque *El Aksa*.

The most remarkable of such substructures are the so-called ' Solomon's Stables ' at the south-east angle of the area. They extend ninety-one yards from east to west, and sixty-six yards from south to north, containing thirteen galleries in all, the vaulting of which is borne by eighty-eight piers in twelve parallel rows. There are also many subsidiary galleries. In this catacomb-like refuge many Jews sought refuge when Jerusalem was captured by the Romans. Most of the vaulting which we can see to-day, however, though built of ancient material and on the ancient site. is of Saracenic construction, and the traces of stable equipment still visible are probably due to the Crusaders. These caverns should not be confused, by the way, with the probably genuine Stables of Solomon recently discovered at Megiddo.*

Mention has been made of the numerous cisterns underlying the Haram area, the holes through which the water was drawn being visible from the surface. They are mentioned by Tacitus,† and must have been familiar objects in New Testament times. One of them is forty feet deep and

* S. L. Caiger : *Bible and Spade*, p. 122.
† Tacitus, Hist. v, 12.

246 yards in circumference, being fed like the Birket Israin and many of the other cisterns by a conduit from the Pools of Solomon some miles to the north of Jerusalem. Beneath it are the usual vaulted chambers, reached by a rock-hewn staircase.

We must now leave the Temple itself and trace its outer walls. Here excavation, though difficult, has not been entirely prohibited, and some assured results have been obtained, chiefly by the laborious method of digging shafts from the surface, and striking out transverse borings deep below the ground towards the original foundations.

An extract from Captain Warren's own description* of such work will give an idea of its difficulty and danger. ' Having dug to a depth of seventy-nine feet, the men were breaking up a stone at the bottom of the shaft, when suddenly the ground gave way, down went the stone and hammer, the men barely saving themselves. They at once rushed up and told the sergeant they had found the bottomless pit.' Warren then describes how he descended the shaft by a thirty-four-foot rope ladder, which was four feet short of the first ledge at which they could pause. Here the rope ladder had to be unhitched, and lowered to the bottom, which again it failed to reach by several feet. ' On reaching the bottom, one recollects that there is still a pit of unknown depth to be explored, and cautiously straddles across it. But after dropping a rope down we find that it is only six feet deep, though it looks black enough for anything.' It must be remembered that all this underground burrowing was accomplished with no better light than tallow candles ! ' Climbing down, we found ourselves in a passage running south from the Haram wall, four feet high by a foot wide, and we crept along it. After advancing for about two

* Quoted in P.E.F., *Our Work in Palestine* (1873).

hundred feet, we found it deep in mud, and had to crawl by means of elbows and toes. Gradually the passage got more and more filled up, till our bodies could barely squeeze through, and there did not appear to be sufficient air to support us for any length of time.' By such methods, where the ground surface is thickly covered with human habitations, sacred buildings, or inviolable cemeteries, has our knowledge of the substructures and general configuration of New Testament Jerusalem been gained.

The only portion of Herod's Temple which may still be seen above ground is the famous ' Wailing Wall ' of the Jews at the south-west angle of the Haram enclosure. Here the lower courses, at any rate, of the lofty wall are clearly of Herodian or perhaps even earlier date, huge roughly-shapen blocks of stone similar to those of ' David's Tower ' —one of them no less than sixteen feet long by thirteen feet wide—too massive for even the Roman battering-ram to disturb. This ancient portion of the wall stretches from the Wailing Place past Robinson's Arch, around the south-west corner, and for some distance along the southern wall. It is a moving thought that upon these very stones, much as we see them to-day, the eyes of Jesus may well have rested, as He foretold the destruction of the Temple. (S. Matthew xxiv, 2.)

For hundreds of years the Jews have gathered at this wall, and do so still. A touching scene is presented by the mournful figures leaning against those weather-beaten stones, kissing them, and weeping aloud for the vanished glories of Israel (see Plate I).

For the Temple that is destroyed, we sit in solitude and mourn ! For the walls that are overthrown, we sit in solitude and mourn ! Haste, haste, Redeemer of Zion ! Speak to the heart of Jerusalem !

To the south of the Wailing Place is an ancient gate, called the *Gate of the Prophet*, or (after its modern discoverer) ' Barclay's Gate.' The upper part of it consists of a huge block, six feet thick and nineteen feet long. The original threshold now lies forty-eight feet below the surface of the ground, where its foundations have been examined. This was evidently the southernmost of the four western gates of the Temple described by Josephus, and thus enables us to ascertain a fixed point in the original wall of Herod's Temple.

South of Barclay's Gate and just before we reach the south-west angle of the enclosure, we come upon the remains of a huge arch called ' Robinson's Arch,' after its discoverer, the first scientific explorer of Jerusalem (1838). Only the spring of this arch, fifty feet in width, and built into the lower temple wall, now survives of the imposing viaduct which once existed—though there are perhaps a few traces of its opposite pier lying fourteen yards away to the west, on the further side of what was once the Tyropœon Valley (Plate IV).

Frequent references to this valley must be made in all descriptions of the topography of Jerusalem. The Tyropœon (Cheesemakers') Valley (so-called by Josephus) was a shallow defile running roughly north-west to south-east through the city, dividing it into two longitudinal halves. It proved troublesome to the architects of ancient days, so was gradually filled up with debris, and is now almost indiscernible.

Robinson's Arch was evidently one of several connecting arches built to span this valley with a causeway which connected the Temple with the western half of the city and with Herod's Palace on the North-West Hill, leading perhaps through the Herodian Xystus, or marble colonnade, of which to-day no certain traces remain. At a depth of forty-two feet below the present surface of the ground, the original pavement of the valley has been discovered with some of the voussoirs (wedge-shaped stones used in shaping an arch-span) still lying upon it as they fell. Most of the ancient stones of Jerusalem, however, have long ago been taken away for use on more recent buildings.

A curious feature of this south-west corner of the Temple area must now be noticed. Originally, and in the earlier temples of Solomon and Zerubbabel, the south-west wall must have swerved inwards so to speak, through the interference of the Tyropœon Valley running athwart it. Herod the Great, however, anxious to complete a true rectangle, partially filled in and partially roofed over the hollow depression with massive vaultings, so that a false plateau was made upon which the new south-west corner of the Temple enclosure could be built, as it is to this day. The original pavement of the valley has been discovered at a depth of thirty-nine feet in places below the present Temple area, and below the pavement still earlier structures have been excavated, including a culverted canal of very early date.

We pass now to the south wall of the Temple, as it was in the days of Herod. This probably followed the line of the present wall, with its Double, Triple, and Single Gates, the first of these being identified with the ' Huldah Gate ' of ancient descriptions, which Jewish tradition asserts to have survived the Destruction of the Temple in A.D. 70. The wall is built of very massive masonry, some of the stones weighing over one hundred tons, which are unlikely to have been disturbed.

The eastern wall of the Temple area, though originally within a parallel city wall, was mainly identical in New Testament times with the fortified wall of the city, built on a rocky scarp dipping steeply into the Kidron Valley. Most of

Plate IV

THE TEMPLE ROCK, VIEWED FROM ABOVE
The oldest altar in the world

(*See page* 65)

HEROD'S VIADUCT OVER THE TYROPŒON
As it looked in the days of Christ

(*See page* 69)

the upper courses of this wall are quite modern, a statement applying also to the ' Golden Gate,' which in its present form dates only from the seventh century A.D. and is thirty feet above the original level of the wall, though probably resting upon an earlier site. The Golden Gate has been blocked up since A.D. 810 by the Arabs on account of the Old Testament prophecy (Ezekiel xliv, 1) that one day a conqueror should enter by this gate.

Coming now to the north-east corner of the Temple, we find the ruins of a massive old tower (sometimes mistakenly called the ' Tower of Antonia '), which dates from New Testament times, or earlier. Builders' marks in red paint have been discovered on the lower stones of this tower, and other points in the more ancient foundations of the Temple, these marks being apparently of Phœnician origin, and connecting us perhaps, with Hiram, King of Tyre, who assisted in the erection of Solomon's Temple.

The course of the north wall is not as clear as one could wish, owing to the indeterminate configuration of the ground and the difficulty of excavation. It is penetrated at several points by underground water courses, very skilfully engineered, which connect the waters of the Birket Israin reservoir just outside the wall with the interior of the Temple.

At the north-west corner of the Temple area, underneath the old Turkish barracks, are the inconsiderable remains of what was once Herod's imposing Castle of Antonia, so named after Mark Antony, which served at once as a fortress against invasion and as a warning to the sometimes unruly Temple lying at its feet. The original Pavement (Gabbatha) of the Herodian central court has recently been discovered, as noted above (see p. 61), near to the Ecce Homo Arch, in the Convent of Our Lady of Sion. The Pavement consists of huge slabs of stone a yard square and

F

a foot or more in thickness, upon which the markings scored
by the Roman soldiery for their games are still visible—
including a game called ' Mocking the King.' There are
also several underground cisterns which supplied the
troops with water. This was the castle out of which
the Roman soldiers ran down to S. Paul's assistance as they
saw him hustled out of the Temple gate below, it was from
the stairs leading up to it that he addressed them in his
defence, and here that he was consigned to his first Roman
prison (Acts xxi, 37). It was also, according to Christian
tradition, the Prætorium whence Christ was led to the Via
Dolorosa and the Cross, as already explained.

Turning southward we follow again the line of the
western wall of the Temple till we come to ' Wilson's Arch.'
This is described by Captain Warren as ' undoubtedly one
of the oldest portions of the sanctuary now existing,' and
preserves one of the original four gates in the Temple wall
mentioned by Josephus. The present arch, which is
Herodian, stands on the site of a still older structure, traces
of which have been found at a depth of twenty-four feet.
Beneath the ground a very elaborate series of vaults has been
found, supporting a viaduct above, and used at one time for
storage, like modern railway arches. A secret passage was
also discovered, connecting the citadel with the Temple, by
which troops could be brought in, and by which, perhaps,
Arabs entered the Temple during the troubles of 1938.
The Gate belonging to Wilson's Arch was the ' Coponius
Gate ' of Jewish tradition, now replaced by an ornamental
gateway made by the Crusaders.

And so we arrive once more where we began our circuit
of the Temple walls, at the Wailing Place of the Jews.
Neither without nor within the walls have we seen very
much to give us a visual impression of the Temple as it

appeared to our Lord. There is not enough left for us even to determine with certainty whether it was built in the Greek style of architecture, like Herod's military and secular buildings, or in the Babylonian style of the Second Temple, or in the mixed Egyptian and Phœnician styles which probably distinguished the original Temple of Solomon. All modern reconstructions of the work, therefore, must be more or less conjectural. But we can form a general idea of its position, plan, and natural surroundings, and feel that here within a few yards is the court where the child Jesus sat amongst the doctors both hearing them and asking them questions (S. Luke ii, 46) or the spot where He overturned the tables of the money-changers and said ' My House is the house of Prayer ' (S. Luke xix, 46).

Only one inscription has survived from New Testament times, a stone plaque which was once attached to the barrier outside the inner Court of Israel, warning Gentiles to venture no farther within the sacred precincts (Plate VII). The inscription runs in Greek as follows* :—

NO STRANGER MAY ENTER WITHIN THE BALUSTRADE ROUND THE TEMPLE AND ENCLOSURE. WHOEVER IS CAUGHT WILL BE RESPONSIBLE TO HIMSELF FOR HIS DEATH, WHICH WILL ENSUE.

The peculiar way in which the penalty for transgression is expressed, indicates that it was not a legal enactment (for the Jews had no right to enforce capital punishment), but rather a warning against the probable consequence of outraging the religious feeling of the populace. It is interesting to note that the word for ' stranger ' (ἀλλογενής) used in this inscription is the very word employed for

* A. Deissmann : *New Light from the Ancient East*, 79 f.

strangers in the New Testament (S. Luke xvii, 18), and in the Septuagint, though never in Classical Greek. So ends our survey of the Holy City. To the archæologist Jerusalem, taken in detail, is an Old Curiosity Shop full of dubious antiques. But taken as a whole, it is as genuine and satisfying a survival from the sacred past as one could hope to find. The atmosphere remains impressively Biblical. To enter Jerusalem, even in these days of changeful modernity, is to leap over the wall of the centuries into the City of David and of David's Son. 'The lanes of Jerusalem are striped like a tiger,' writes Morton,* ' You pass perpetually from strips of sunlight into bands of shadow.' He sees the city still as it was 1900 years ago—furtively ferocious, beautifully cruel, intolerant as ever. ' This,' he feels, ' is undoubtedly the place which crucified Jesus Christ.'

* H. V. Morton : *Steps of the Master.*

V

SACRED SITES OF PALESTINE

SO far we have followed the footsteps of Christ within the circumference of the Holy City or in its immediate neighbourhood ; we must now follow them farther afield, to the hill country of Judæa, to Galilee of the Gentiles, to the coasts of Tyre and Sidon, and wherever the Gospel story leads us in the Holy Land. It must be remembered that the visits of our Lord to Jerusalem were those of a comparative stranger to the city, short and infrequent, the greater part of His life, including His three years' ministry, being spent in Galilee and the North. A survey of Palestine as a whole, therefore, is essential to our understanding of His environment.

THE MOUNT OF OLIVES

In the day time He was teaching in the Temple ; and at night He went out, and abode in the mount that is called the Mount of Olives.—(S. Luke xxi, 37.)

East of Jerusalem on the farther side of the Kidron Valley, the Mount of Olives still preserves some of the most sacred associations of our Lord's earthly sojourn, especially in connection with the last days of His ministry. From this vantage point He looked down upon the Temple and foresaw its coming destruction ; down these gentle slopes He rode meek and lowly upon an ass on His last entry into the city ; and here after the Last Supper He sought the solitude of the Garden of Gethsemane, where He was betrayed.

At the foot of the Mount of Olives the ' Garden of Gethsemane ' is still preserved by the Franciscans on a site which goes back to the fourth century, and which agrees in all particulars with the Gospel narrative. Of the olive trees which once covered the hill only eight remain, eight venerable trees split by age and shored up with earth and stones, yet still bearing fruit. Here is the ' Cavern of the Agony,' hollowed in the living rock, which must have been, if not the actual scene of His agonised prayer, at least a familiar object to Him as He passed this way two thousand years ago.

Many other incidents of our Lord's life are commemorated on this historic hill—there is a Chapel of the Ascension, the Tomb of the Virgin, the Tombs of Joachim and Anne, the spot where Jesus wept over the City, the place where He appeared to the Men of Galilee after the Resurrection, the Church of the Lord's Prayer (now inscribed with that Prayer in thirty-two different languages), the place where Jesus met Martha, and so on. But these traditions mostly date from the Crusading era, and have little historic probability behind them. The so-called ' Tombs of the Prophets,' a series of old rock-tombs of early Jewish type, may have been existent in New Testament times, though afterwards adapted for Christian burials in the fourth to sixth centuries.

It will be convenient now to mention the other sacred sites of Palestine in their alphabetical order.

BETHANY AND BETHPHAGE

When He was come nigh to Bethphage and Bethany, at the mount called the Mount of Olives, He sent two of His disciples saying, Go ye into the village over against you.—(S. Luke xix, 29.)

Bethany, where our Lord was anointed by the woman with the alabaster box of ointment, and where He raised Lazarus, brother of Mary and Martha from the dead, lay on the eastern slope of the Mount of Olives. Its true site is unquestionably to be found at the modern village whose Arabic name, *El-Azariyeh* (Place of Lazarus), preserves the ancient tradition that here the raising of Lazarus took place. The underground cavern shown as the ' Tomb of Lazarus ' was formerly a rock chamber with burial niches in vaulted recesses on three sides, and almost certainly dates from New Testament times. Archæological discoveries have proved, too, that a village stood on this spot before the Christian era.

Of the village of Bethphage no certain traces have been found.

BETHLEHEM

And Joseph also went up from Galilee, out of the city of Nazareth, into Judæa, unto the city of David, which is called Bethlehem.—(S. Luke ii, 4.)

One of the oldest and best authenticated Holy Places in Palestine is the Church of the Nativity in Bethlehem and the Grotto of the Nativity which it enshrines. Even before the erection of the ancient church on this spot, Origen (A.D. 248)* quotes an earlier Father of the Church, Justin Martyr (born about A.D. 100), as his authority for identifying the celebrated grotto in Bethlehem with the actual birthplace of our Lord. *Should anyone desire other proof*, wrote Justin, *for the birth of Jesus in Bethlehem according to Micah's prophecy and the history described by the disciples in the Gospels, let him consider that, in harmony with the Gospel story of His birth, a cave*

* Origen : *Against Celsus*, i, 51.

is shown in Bethlehem where He was born, and the manger in the cave where He lay wrapped in swaddling clothes. As a matter of strict accuracy, the New Testament does not say He was born in a *cave*, but that the tradition is extremely early is proved by its unquestioned appearance in the early Apocryphal Gospels such as the *Protevangelium of S. James.**

It is as certain as anything of this nature can be that the grotto now pointed out as the Birthplace of Jesus is the same cave as that which was so honoured by pilgrims in those early days of Christendom, which Hadrian was said to have desecrated by superimposing on it a Temple of Adonis, and over which Constantine built his Church of the Nativity as early as A.D. 326.

The Church which now rises south of old Bethlehem upon this sacred spot is undoubtedly one of the oldest in the world, though of course it has suffered alteration through the centuries. Of the original three entrance doors built by the Roman Emperor, or rather by his mother, S. Helena,† a small wicket-gate in the centre still remains, the lintel deliberately built so low that one has to stoop, bowing the head in reverence as it were, before entering this holy place. (Plate V). The entrances at each side of this wicket-gate are blocked up. Thence a dark vestibule leads into the wide nave of the Roman basilica, which, surviving almost intact, gives us the best possible example of the earliest type of Christian church. A double row of Corinthian columns divides the church into aisles each side of the nave, the roof having been covered at one time with English lead imported by Edward IV, probably from the Royal mines at Wirksworth.

The usual shape of a basilica is plain oblong, like the

* This may be found in R. James : *The Apocryphal New Testament.*
† Eusebius : *Life of Constantine* iii, 41.

synagogues in which the earliest Christians worshipped, but in this case we find the basilica has acquired an almost cruciform shape, owing to the architect's desire to include within the transept both the Grotto of the Nativity, and plenty of room for a crowd of pilgrims at each side. As early as A.D. 333 the celebrated ' Bordeaux Pilgrim ' describes a visit to this shrine, and many archæologists hold that the church which stands in Bethlehem to-day is the same in all essentials as that which Constantine originally built.

Once again we may quote the ecstatic description of Sophronius*: *Subduing the excessive fervour of sacred love which would burn in my heart, I would go straightway to that little village of Bethlehem, wherein the Lord of all was born and passing through the noble portico of four columns into the midst of that most splendid triple-vaulted building, I would dance for very joy. . . . I would view the grotto wherein the Virgin Queen of all brought forth the Saviour of all mortal men. Upon the famous floor whereon the Child God was placed, I would press my eyes, my mouth, and my forehead, that I might bear away from thence a blessing. . . .*

From the transept of this church two flights of steps descend into the cave or Chapel of the Nativity, forty feet long and twelve feet wide, the walls now being lined with marble. In front of the canopied altar is a squared recess with a silver star let into the pavement inscribed (in Latin) : ' Jesus Christ was born here of the Virgin Mary.' From the roof of the recess hang fifteen ever-lighted lamps—the ' silver lamps on a distant shrine ' of the well-known Christmas carol.

Opposite this are three steps leading down to the Chapel of the Manger, where a slab of stone containing a concave oval holds at Christmastide a wax model of the Holy Child.

* Quoted in G. Dalman : *Sacred Sites and Ways* p. 55.

There are also other memorial chapels in the vicinity, commemorating the Adoration of the Wise Men, the Slaughter of the Innocents, and so on. At a little distance from the church stands the Milk Grotto, a natural cavern where the Blessed Virgin is said to have suckled her Child, and where the limestone dust is still believed to be helpful to nursing mothers.

About two miles out of the town is the Tomb of Rachel, a small building of ancient construction now domed, which was already revered by the Jews in the time of Christ, and must have been a familiar object to Him. At a greater distance is the Field of the Shepherds, containing an ancient cavern where the Angels are said to have appeared to them on Christmas morning.

Such fanciful traditions apart, there seems to be no good reason for doubting that the Grotto of the Nativity may be the true birthplace of our Lord. In that case the cave must originally have served as a stable for an inn built over it or in its proximity. Hither, when ' there was no room for them in the inn,' the Virgin was conducted, and on the manger in this stable she laid her Child. Even to this day in Palestine there is nothing unusual in the rocky niche with its simple hollowed manger which we see in the Chapel of the Manger, and pre-Christian examples of this type have been found.

Nor is there anything strange in the suggestion of mediæval representations of the Nativity showing the Holy Family surrounded by the cattle which ordinarily occupied the stable. For in Palestine to-day the dwelling-place of man and beast is often in the same room—though the house is usually cleared for a woman in childbirth. To this day there are many primitive houses in Bethlehem which remind one of the old Christmas story. These houses are built over caves, the cave being level with the road, and used for stabling cattle, while a stone stairway leads to the living rooms above. Perhaps the old inn at Bethlehem was built in this way.

Of archæological proof of the genuineness of this site there is, of course, and can be, none. Perhaps the whole matter may be best summed up in the words of Professor G. Dalman,* one of the leading authorities on the subject : ' The most ancient local tradition out of which the Church of Bethlehem grew is, after all, not necessarily authentic, but yet it may quite well have hit upon the truth. The grotto under the church, with its manger, may not be the exact spot where Christ was born. But, at any rate, a hundred years after the Crucifixion it is with Bethlehem, the city of David, that the mystery of Christ's birth was connected, and, at the same time, it is the oldest firmly-established place of His veneration.' Dalman also points out that in this Church of the Holy Nativity originated the universally popular custom of keeping ' Merry Christmas ' in honour of the Holy Babe, the original date, however, being January 6, the Feast of the Epiphany Star.

BETHSAIDA

He went aside privately into a desert place belonging to the city called Bethsaida.—(S. Luke ix, 10.)

The birthplace of Peter, Andrew and Philip, which is connected also with the Feeding of the Five Thousand (S. Luke ix, 10) has been located under the modern village of *El Tell* on the east of the Lake of Galilee. It was rebuilt by Philip the Tetrarch, son of Herod the Great, and renamed Julias in honour of the daughter of Augustus. The ruins

* G. Dalman : *Sacred Sites and Ways*, p. 45.

now consist only of a few ancient fragments, chiefly of basalt thickly covered with thistles.

CÆSAREA PHILIPPI

When Jesus came into the coasts of Cæsarea Philippi, He asked His disciples, saying, Whom do men say that I the Son of Man am?—(S. Matthew xvi, 13.)

The scene of S. Peter's great confession, modern *Banias*, lies high amongst the hills of Mount Hermon.   The remains of a sanctuary of Pan erected by Herod the Great are still visible, as noted above (p. 47).   On the rocks, still half legible, are Greek inscriptions of the days of Agrippa, one dedicating an altar to the Nymphs, another recording the name of Agrippa as archon of the year, and so on.   But the cave of Pan has now collapsed, so that the sudden spouting of water which so struck the imagination of Josephus is no longer remarkable.

CANA

The third day there was a marriage in Cana of Galilee ; and the mother of Jesus was there.—(S. John ii, 1.)

The village where Jesus wrought His first miracle of changing water into wine is usually identified with *Kafr Kenna*, north-east of Nazareth.   There is a synagogue here, preserving perhaps some very early remains, and said to occupy the spot where the miracle was performed.   Some, however, would identify it rather with *Khirbet Kana*, some miles due north of Nazareth, in accordance with a persistent tradition dating back to the fifth century.   There are no significant remains in this village, but not far away is the so-called Tomb of Hiram. which must have been a

conspicuous object to our Lord as He walked on the road
to Tyre and Sidon. This ancient Phœnician monument
consists of a pedestal of huge stones over which is suspended
an enormous slab of rock, bearing a massive sarcophagus
covered with a pyramidal lid of stone about twenty feet high.

CAPERNAUM

*He came down to Capernaum, a city of Galilee, and taught
them on the Sabbath days.*—(S. Luke iv, 31.)

Capernaum, on the shores of the Lake of Tiberias, was
the headquarters of Christ in His Galilean ministry. Here
He healed the servant of the centurion who had built a
synagogue for the Jews (S. Luke vii, 5) and in that synagogue
He often preached. Although once a town of considerable
importance, its site has been a matter of dispute, some
preferring *Khan Minyeh* on the north-west shores of the
lake, while the majority of modern archæologists elect for
Tell Hum, about three miles farther north along the shore,
where the remains appear to be more ancient than those of
Khan Minyeh. The name Capernaum appears to be a
corruption of the form found in the Jewish Talmud *Caphar
Tanhum*, or Tomb of Tanhum, the latter in its turn being
corrupted to *Telhum*, and by a false analogy *Tell Hum*, the
Mound of Hum. It has, however, been ingeniously
suggested (with reference to S. Matthew, who sat at the
receipt of custom in this place) that Telhum is an Arabic
corruption of Telonium (Greek τελώνιον), or Customs
House.

The site of Tell Hum fits in well with the Gospel allusions
to Capernaum, and it has been a resort of pilgrims from the
fourth century. The ruins of a Byzantine church, which
was evidently intended to commemorate the sacred spot,

were discovered by Orfali in 1921. Of town walls there is no trace, and the many loose stones found upon the site are too disconnected to prove more than the existence at one time of a quarrying and stone-mason's industry in this place. There is also a cemetery containing tombs of the Roman period which may have been known to our Lord, including one rather unusual sepulchre hewn underground in the solid rock, probably identifiable with the 'Tomb of Nahum' venerated by the Jews in ancient times.

But the most notable ruin in *Tell Hum* is the famous Synagogue of Capernaum, which is unequalled for preservation, beauty, and interest among all such remains in Western Palestine. As an example of the sort of building in which Christ and His contemporaries worshipped, this synagogue must be of paramount interest to the New Testament archæologist ; while if we consider that it may be the actual synagogue which was built by the Roman centurion, and in which Christ Himself preached so often on the Sabbath days of twenty centuries ago, the interest we feel is naturally increased. Since 1925 the ruin has been in the possession of the Franciscans, who have partially restored it, as seen in our photograph (Plate V).

Before discussing the date and identification of these remains, however, it will be best to describe them. The building is of white limestone, richly carved and ornamented. The ruins are complete enough to make a full reconstruction of the original synagogue possible. There were three doors side by side on the ground floor, the central door the largest, looking south towards the Galilean Lake. At the farther end of this same south wall was a flight of stone stairs leading to a small landing, with another door opening upon the upper story. The lintels of the doors were square, not overarched, and were heavily ornamented with carved reliefs of animals, birds, beasts and foliage. One of the most interesting representations is that of the Ark of the Covenant, a convex-lidded chest on four wheels. On an original keystone, for instance, two eagles face each other, and there are representations of a manna-pot, a Passover Lamb, palm trees, vines, wreaths of flowers and leaves. Some quaint animals amongst the carvings have been identified as centaurs, half-horse half-human figures of pagan mythology !

That such florid and pictorial decoration should have been permitted in a Jewish synagogue, came as a shock to archæologists, who expected the Jews of these early centuries to be more scrupulous in their observance of the Commandment against making ' graven images ' or ' the likeness of anything in heaven or earth ' (Exodus xx, 4). It was even suggested that here could be seen an additional proof that the synagogue was built by a Gentile, the centurion of S. Luke vii, 5, his pagan taste in decoration being overlooked in virtue of his munificence. But it seems that the strictness with which the Second Commandment was kept varied greatly in different periods. In 4 B.C. the golden eagle erected by Herod in the Temple was pulled down with howls of execration, and in A.D. 66 the Palace of Herod Antipas in Tiberias was destroyed because of the pictures of animals on its walls. But in later times such severity was exceptional, Rabbinic law expressly permitting such representations, excluding only the human figure. Graven images of one sort or another, in fact, are extremely common upon Palestinian synagogues of the third century and onwards.*

A word must here be said about the many synagogue ruins of ancient date still to be found in Palestine, for by a

* ' Iconic decoration, far from being exceptional, was characteristic of the Roman and Byzantine periods corresponding to the age of the Talmud,' W. F. Albright : *The Archæology of Palestine and the Bible* (2nd Edit. , 1933), p. 58.

comparison of these ruins we are enabled to reconstruct what would otherwise be lacking in the Capernaum synagogue.* They all have certain normal features—a triple doorway, often facing south ; rows of pillars within an oblong cross-section ; emblematical representations of ' Solomon's Seal ' (interlaced triangles) ; stone benches round the walls ; and ornamentation in stone relief showing such designs as the seven-branched candlestick, the cup of manna, vine leaves and grapes; palm trees, eagles, doves and all sorts of animals, especially lions.   Occasionally there are human figures, but these, like the eagles, have generally been mutilated.   There are even pictorial representations of Biblical scenes, like Daniel in the Lions' Den, and the Sacrifice of Isaac.   There was usually an outer court, with a raised terrace mounted by steps, and it is probable that there were interior galleries supported by wooden beams.

Synagogues of early date, showing the above characteristics, have been excavated at many places.   At Jericho in 1929 Crowfoot discovered an ancient synagogue which had been converted into a Christian church.   Under the floor was found a mosaic of the Flood, with the names of Shem and Japheth in Greek, depicting processions of animals, birds and reptiles entering the Ark, also the dove with its olive branch.   An inscription in Hebrew read : *Amen ; Sela ; Peace be to the synagogue.   Peace be upon all Israel.   Amen.   Amen*, together with the names of the builders : *Phinehas son of Rabbi Baruch, Joseph son of Rabbi Samuel, Judah son of Rabbi Hezekiah*.   The date of this building was about A.D. 400, but it undoubtedly repeated an earlier building tradition.   Similar ruined synagogues have been found at *Kerazeh*, see Chorazin below ;   at

---

* It is generally agreed amongst archæologists that not a single surviving synagogue belongs actually to the New Testament period.   The first century synagogues were all destroyed, if not by Titus in A.D. 68, then by Hadrian in A.D. 135.

Irbid (Arbela) on the lake facing east ; at *Khirbet Ummel Amed ;* and at *Kefr Birim*, between Safed and Tyre, where the Tomb of Esther is pointed out. At the latter site an inscription was discovered reading : *Peace be upon this place and all the places of Israel. Joseph the Levite the son of Levi put up this lintel. A blessing rest upon his work.* Other synagogue remains have been found at *El Jish* (Gischala), two miles south of the above ; at *Meron*, the burial place of the famous Rabbis Hillel and Shammai ; at *Nebratain*, where a perfect lintel with a cryptic Hebrew inscription is preserved ; and at many other spots.

Returning to the synagogue at Capernaum, its interior was oblong, seventy-nine feet long by fifty-nine feet wide, resembling a basilica without the apse—the typical basilica-design exhibited in the churches of the early Christians being probably conditioned by the construction of the synagogues in which they first worshipped. There seems to have been a double-floored colonnade built round three sides, the upper floor being intended for the women. The pillars of the lower colonnade have debased Corinthian capitals, and are mounted on high plinths. A fragment from one of these pillars anticipates some modern places of worship, in recording that particular parts of the synagogue were bestowed by certain named individuals—one of them being called *Zebedee the son of John !* (Was he, one wonders, a descendant of the scriptural John the son of Zebedee ?) Double stone benches ran along each side-wall for the worshippers.

The dais or rostrum in this synagogue probably stood against an ornamental wall, parts of which remain. It is evident from the general design of the building that the congregation were intended to face south, that is towards Jerusalem, whilst at prayer. A large window in the south

G

side supplied the necessary light for the reading of the Law and the Prophets, the rolls of which must have been kept in a special chest.

On the eastern side of the synagogue was a court with a three-sided colonnade, together with a stairway, of which ten steps remain, leading up to the platform above. Possibly a basin stood here for the purpose of washing the feet of worshippers. Three stone vessels, apparently for water, have been found, reminding us of the ' water-pots of stone ' filled by our Lord at Cana. (John ii, 6.)

As to the date of this remarkable building, it seems impossible to be quite certain. Meistermann, Orfali and others believe it to be of the Herodian period, and are certain it was the synagogue built by the centurion. There are several references in the Jewish records to benefactions made by pious Gentiles to synagogues, although no mention has been found of the donation of a complete synagogue, with the exception of this passage in S. Luke vii. The disfigurement of some of the pictorial representations on this synagogue is ascribed to the outburst of fanaticism at the time of the Jewish rebellion in A.D. 66. Kohl and Watzinger, on the other hand, having excavated here in 1905, detected several marks of third-century work amongst the remains, and consider that the synagogue was built by order of the Emperor Antoninus Pius about A.D. 200. Other scholars would date it even later. But whatever the date of the actual ruins now extant, there is general agreement that the synagogue was built upon a previously existing site, and in accordance with a long-established architectural tradition.

Dalman* sums up as follows : ' Taking all into considera- tion, we are on safe ground when we regard the synagogue

* G. Dalman : *Sacred Sites and Ways*, p. 152.

of *Tell Hum*, which we hope will never be rebuilt, as a reconstruction of that in which Jesus healed one possessed (S. Luke iv, 33) and restored the withered arm of another sufferer (S. Luke vi, 6). . . . It is impossible to determine with certainty the exact site of all these places. But there is no spot in the whole of Palestine where memories heap themselves up to such an extent as in Capernaum.'

CHORAZIN

*Woe unto thee, Chorazin ! Woe unto thee, Bethsaida !
For if the mighty works had been done in Tyre and Sidon,
which have been done in you, they had a great while ago
repented, sitting in sackcloth and ashes. But it shall be more
tolerable for Tyre and Sidon at the Judgment, than for you.—*
(S. Luke x, 13, 14.)

Two miles to the north of Capernaum, up in the hills, lie the ruins of Chorazin, now *Kerazeh*, of which we gather from the denunciation quoted above that our Lord preached there His Gospel of the Kingdom, and preached in vain.

Here on the summit of an eighty-foot cliff are the ruins of another ancient Jewish synagogue, built of the native black basalt, and richly ornamented with sculptures. Among these we see the animals, centaurs and grape clusters already noted at Capernaum. The name of a certain *Judan son of Ishmael* is inscribed on one of the seats as a benefactor to the synagogue. Again we find the usual three doors in the gable-side looking towards the south, and the double-floored colonnade within the interior. Traces of the old Roman road from Capernaum to this up-country village still remain.

EMMAUS

*And, behold, two of them went that same day to a village
called Emmaus, which was from Jerusalem about threescore
furlongs.*—(S. Luke xxiv, 13.)

The site of Emmaus, where Cleopas and his friend
begged the Risen Lord to ' abide with us, for it is toward
evening, and the day is far spent,' has not been identified
with any degree of certainty.   Though the name is similar,
the site cannot have been at *Amwas* on the main Jerusalem-
Jaffa road (the Emmaus-Nicopolis where Judas Maccabæus
defeated Gorgias), for this is over eightscore furlongs from
Jerusalem, which, besides disagreeing with the distance
given in S. Luke's Gospel, is rather far for an afternoon
walk from the city.

Since the fifteenth century, the New Testament Emmaus
has been located at *El Kubeibeh*, just over threescore furlongs
from Jerusalem.   Here are the ruins of an ancient house
called the House of Cleopas, which was once enclosed within
a Byzantine church.   But the name Emmaus (*Hamma*)
implies the existence of hot springs of which there are none
in this neighbourhood.   On neither site are there any certain
first-century remains.   A better case has been made out for
Artas (=Hortus) near Bethlehem.*

GADARA, GERASA, GERGESA

*And they arrived at the country of the Gadarenes, which is
over against Galilee. . . .   Then went the devils out of the
man, and entered into the swine ; and the herd ran violently
down a steep place into the lake, and were choked.*—(S. Luke
viii, 26-33.)

The name of the small village on the shores of the Galilean
Lake where our Lord suffered the evil spirits to pass into

* P.E.F.Q., 1883, p. 53.

the herd of swine, was so unfamiliar to the evangelists that the spelling varies : Gadara, Gerasa, or Gergesa. Of these Gadara (*Umkes*) and Gerasa (*Jerash*) were miles away from the lake, so that probably the correct spelling of the name is Gergesa, modern *Kersa*, on the eastern shores. A mile to the south of this spot is a steep slope running almost straight into the sea. There are no ancient remains.

Gerasa, the modern *Jerash*, is not mentioned in the New Testament, except possibly by a misunderstanding as noted above. It was not, indeed, until A.D. 65, the year of S. Paul's imprisonment in Rome, that Gerasa was rebuilt by the Romans, and attained a brief five years of butterfly brilliance before it was destroyed during the suppression of the Jewish rebellion in A.D. 70. Rebuilt early in the second century, it attained its highest peak of prosperity under Hadrian and Trajan. Its interest for New Testament students lies mainly, therefore, in the impression given by its exceptionally well-preserved and extensive remains of a typical, though not actually first-century, Græco-Roman city of Palestine.

To the south of the town stands a handsome Triumphal Gate twenty-four feet wide and thirty-nine feet high, strikingly like the celebrated Triumphal Arch of Trajan in Rome commemorating the Fall of Jerusalem. Remains of a vast amphitheatre, with an artificial basin for nautical spectacles and an aqueduct to supply it, are still visible surrounded by tiers of seats. The ruins of a noble Temple, with columns and column-bases still existing, adjoin a great Theatre with its seating arrangements still remarkably preserved. The Market Place presents a most striking appearance with its semicircular enclosure of fifty-six Ionic columns largely intact. From this leads the celebrated *Via Principalis*, forty-one feet wide, with seventy-five of its graceful Corinthian columns still standing guard. A second Temple, with its broad stairway and colonnaded portico of perfectly preserved columns forty-five feet high, was probably dedicated to the Sun-god. And there are other similar remains, making Jerash in many ways the most satisfying site in Palestine from a general archæological point of view.

GAZA AND AZOTUS

The angel of the Lord spake unto Philip, saying, Arise, and go toward the south unto the way that goeth down from Jerusalem unto Gaza, which is desert.—(Acts viii, 26.)

The site of ancient Gaza, on the road to which Philip the Deacon encountered and baptized the Ethiopian eunuch, is well known to-day as *Ghazzeh ;* it is, in fact, still an important town. The Gaza of Old Testament times had been destroyed by Alexander Jannæus in 96 B.C. but rebuilt some distance to the south of the former site, and presented by Augustus to Herod the Great.

Little is left of the Herodian town except the outline of the ancient walls, all the original masonry having been used up in two thousand years of subsequent building, after the economical manner of Palestine. An isolated column in the Great Mosque here, containing a bas-relief representing the seven-branched candlestick with a Greek and Hebrew inscription, may be an ancient survival. The most interesting remains at Gaza, recently excavated by Sir Flinders Petrie, belong to Old Testament times, and do not concern us here.

A similar absence of early remains has to be noted at *Esdud*, the Ashdod or Azotus of the Bible, whither Philip journeyed after the baptism of the eunuch (Acts viii, 40).

At *Askalan* (Ashkelon), however, where Herod the Great was born, many striking ruins of the Herodian period may still be seen—some fortified walls, with gates and towers deeply buried in sand.

JERICHO

A certain man went down from Jerusalem to Jericho, and fell among thieves.—(S. Luke x, 30.)

The site of Jericho, associated in the Gospel story with blind Bartimæus, with the rich little publican Zacchæus, and with the parable of the Good Samaritan, lay near the modern *El Richa* in the Jordan Valley five miles north of the Dead Sea. The adjacent mound has become famous of recent years on account of Garstang's epoch-making excavations, and the discovery of the ancient city destroyed by Joshua in 1400 B.C.*

New Testament Jericho had been largely rebuilt before the birth of Jesus by Herod the Great, with a magnificent citadel, hippodrome and other buildings in the usual Græco-Roman style. But all this splendour had disappeared by the fourth century.

The old Roman 'road from Jerusalem to Jericho,' however, still remains much as it was in the days of the Good Samaritan, a road of hairpin bends, overhanging cliffs, and hundreds of natural caverns where bandits have lurked from time immemorial. On the crest of a ridge in the road still stands the so-called ' Inn of the Good Samaritan,' the ancient foundations and sunken rock cisterns of which prove it to have stood on this site, the only khan on the road, from at least first-century times. It is a single-storied stone building, roofed with red tiles,

* S. L. Caiger : *Bible and Spade*, p. 95f.

standing at one side of a large enclosed courtyard, and dominated from an adjacent mound by the ruins of a Crusader's Castle.

JOPPA

Now there was at Joppa a certain disciple named Tabitha, which by interpretation is called Dorcas.—(Acts ix, 36.)

Joppa, where S. Peter restored Tabitha to life and where he received Cornelius in the house of Simon the Tanner, is still, under the modern name of Jaffa, a considerable seaport and the centre of the orange-growing industry of Palestine. S. Peter's Joppa was destroyed by Vespasian in A.D. 68, and very few traces of the ancient town survive, though several New Testament sites, such as the House of Simon the Tanner, are pointed out to pilgrims.

LYDDA

Forasmuch as Lydda was nigh to Joppa, and the disciples had heard that Peter was there, they sent unto him two men, desiring him that he would not delay to come to them.—(Acts ix, 38.)

Lydda, the Lod of the Old Testament, where S. Peter healed Æneas, was destroyed by Cestius Gallus not many years after the incident recorded above. It revived, however, and is still, under the name of *Ludd*, an inhabited town. There are no remains of an earlier date than the Crusades.

MACHÆRUS

But when Herod's birthday was kept, the daughter of Herodias danced before them, and pleased Herod. . . . And he sent, and beheaded John in the prison.—(S. Matthew xiv, 6, 10.)

Machærus is not mentioned by name in the New Testament, but according to Josephus it was the place where Herod Antipas imprisoned and beheaded the Baptist. The fortress here was one of the last to be reduced by the Romans in the Jewish War, and its ruins still survive, at *Mukaur* east of the Dead Sea, in the shape of a massive tower and large cisterns, which give some impression of the ancient strength of Herod's chief fortress. Amongst the ruins is an underground dungeon where the Baptist is reputed to have been imprisoned.

MASADA

The mountain stronghold of Masada, now *Es-Sebbeh*, is not named in the Bible, but is a place of tragic association with New Testament times. It was fortified by Herod the Great, who enclosed the whole plateau on the summit of the hill with a white stone wall furnished with thirty-seven towers. After the destruction of Jerusalem in A.D. 70 the Jews made their last stand here against the Romans, until at last in despair they and their families committed mass suicide.

Ruins of the towers may still be seen, as also the remains of the Roman embankment erected against the Jewish fortress. Photographs taken from the air reveal a perfectly clear and complete outline of the square Roman camp from which the besiegers attacked this last stronghold of militant Judaism.

NAZARETH

And He came to Nazareth, where He had been brought up.
—(S. Luke iv, 16.)

It was in this obscure village in northern Galilee that the Annunciation of the coming birth of Christ was made to the Blessed Virgin, and here during the greater part of His life lived Jesus of Nazareth, the carpenter, until at length ' they thrust Him out of the city ' because of His preaching.

To-day *En Nasira* is no longer an insignificant village, but a large town with several industries besides that of entertaining the countless pilgrims who visit the Home of the Holy Family. Many sacred sites are shown, such as the Church of the Annunciation, the spot from which the Loretto House of the Virgin was transported to Italy, the Workshop of Joseph, the Table of Christ (*Mensa Christi*), and so on.

One, at any rate, of the Holy Places of Nazareth must be well authenticated, namely S. Mary's Well, for it is, and apparently always has been, the only well in the place, and as all the women stream up to it to-day with their pitchers on their heads or under their arms, so the Blessed Virgin must have waited her turn at this very well. It has been called S. Mary's Well (*Ain Miriam*) since the eleventh century, and is situated near the Church of Gabriel, the Angel of the Annunciation.

Other remains of some archæological importance are those of an ancient Synagogue, now restored as a Greek Uniat Church, on the present market-road. An area covered over with a barrel-vaulting is shown as the School of the Messiah, and may be part of the Nazareth synagogue where the Holy Child learnt His letters. Four rectangular blocks with Hebrew letters inscribed upon them, found nearby, may have belonged to this building. Of these remains Dalman* writes : ' It is not impossible that in the time of Christ the Synagogue stood on the same spot. Hence the synagogue church is for us the most important of the memorial sites of Nazareth.'

SAMARIA

Then Philip went down to the city of Samaria, and preached Christ unto them. And the people with one accord gave heed unto those things which Philip spake.—(Acts viii, 5, 6.)

The site of the ancient city of Samaria, scene of S. Philip's preaching, and chief city of the country of the Samaritans through which our Lord passed on His way from Galilee to Jerusalem, is still covered by extensive and imposing remains of the New Testament period. Below these lie the foundations of that older Samaria, which was fortified by Omri and Ahab as the capital of the Northern Kingdom, and where recent excavation has discovered the splendid palace of the Kings of Israel with many of its famous ivories and inscribed potsherds still intact.†

In New Testament times this city was presented by the Emperor Augustus to Herod the Great, who rebuilt it and called it after his patron, Sebaste (Greek for Augusta), the name being still preserved in the modern *Sebastiyeh*, which stands on the ancient site. The magnificent palace, temple, hippodrome, and towering fortifications of Sebaste must have been a familiar spectacle to the first Christians, reminding them, perhaps, of the godless Samaria of Old Testament times, whose Fall (in 722 B.C.) had been so sternly prophesied by Amos and Hosea.

* G. Dalman : *Sacred Sites and Ways*, p. 68.
† S. L. Caiger : *Bible and Spade*, p. 134.

On the top of the hill the ground plan of Herod's Temple of Augustus can be clearly defined, access to it being gained by a great marble staircase, of which two flights of twelve steps each, over seventy feet in width, still convey some impression of former magnificence. A Roman altar has been found among the ruins, and near to it a colossal marble statue of the ' Divine ' Augustus himself. On the west of the hill a massive Roman gate flanked by two round towers superimposed on more ancient squared foundations and another tower at the south-west corner, help one to visualize the strength of the ancient walls.

The outline of built-up terraces surrounding the hill can still be seen, and leading from the western to the eastern gate is one of the most impressive examples of a Herodian *Via Principalis* existing in Palestine. Many of the columns are still standing along the line of a colonnade fully a mile in length and twenty yards in width, the columns being over sixteen feet in height. To the north-east of the hill are more broken columns, and the ruins of a typical Greek stadium. On the west have been discovered the foundations of a colonnaded hall adjoining the ancient market place. At very few places in Palestine can one get a better impression of the appearance of a typical Græco-Roman city of the New Testament era.

SYCHAR

Then cometh He to a city of Samaria, which is called Sychar, near to the parcel of ground that Jacob gave to his son Joseph. Now Jacob's well was there.—(S. John iv, 5.)

Sychar, near to the well where Jesus spoke with the Woman of Samaria, may perhaps be located at the mound *Tulul Balata*, half a mile west of the well known as Jacob's, rather than at Shechem (Neapolis, *Nablus*) or at *Askar*, which are too far distant. At *Balata* some existing remains show that a village stood on the spot in Roman times.

There can be little doubt as to the identification of Jacob's Well, accredited by an unbroken tradition for many centuries. This well lies on a crossing of the highroad from Jerusalem to Galilee (as implied in the Gospel narrative) and the main road from Sebaste to Peræa. It is the first roadside well on the journey from Jerusalem to the north, and a natural resting place for the traveller's midday meal. It lies at the foot of Mount Gerizim, the sacred mountain of the Samaritans, so that, passing here to-day, one can look up at the towering summit three thousand feet above, and picture the Woman of Samaria pointing out the hill to Jesus as she said : ' Our fathers worshipped in this mountain.' (S. John iv, 20.)

The opening of the well now lies in the crypt of a Crusaders' Chapel, erected on the ruins of a fourth-century commemorative shrine. The cistern, over seven feet in diameter, can alas ! no longer be depended upon for water in summer-time owing to the rubbish which has been allowed to accumulate in it—though it is still over seventy feet in depth.

TIBERIAS

After these things Jesus went over the sea of Galilee, which is the sea of Tiberias.—(S. John vi, 1.)

Apart from an isolated reference in S. John's Gospel (vi, 23), this city is entirely ignored by the writers of the New Testament, and apparently was never visited by our Lord. How little one would guess that in the time of Christ it was actually the official capital of the important tetrarchy of

Galilee, a city of the first rank both in magnificence and size ! It is more than probable that this contemptuous silence was deliberate. While Jesus was still at work in the carpenter's shop at Nazareth, all Galilee must have hummed with the story of how Herod Antipas had sacrilegiously disturbed the graves of a Jewish cemetery when digging the foundations of his new capital in A.D. 21. In consequence, though it was completed seven years before the Crucifixion, with every attraction known to Roman art and civilization, no Jew in our Lord's day could ever bring himself to enter the accursed place. Yet strange to relate, it became after the Fall of Jerusalem in A.D. 70, the chief centre of orthodox Judaism in the world.

To-day *Tabariya* shows few signs of its former glory. ' It is a shabby, squalid little town,' writes H. V. Morton, ' and crouches like a beggar on the lakeside. It is a town of rags and dark eyes and dark cellars, of little jumbled shops and narrow streets.' On the north, however, are the extensive ruins of a large castle originally built by Herod Antipas, and part of his three-mile wall can still be traced. His palace is marked only by heaps of black basalt masonry and a few shattered pillars. The celebrated hot spring of mineral waters, mentioned by the classical writers, still gushes from a hillside south of the town, on the way to which one passes the remains of a massive Herodian wall, some broken columns, and the ruins of a fine aqueduct.

TYRE AND SIDON

Again, departing from the coasts of Tyre and Sidon, He came unto the Sea of Galilee.—(S. Mark vii, 31.)

Though it was in the neighbourhood of Tyre and Sidon that Christ healed the daughter of the woman who ' was a

Greek, a Syro-Phœnician by nation,' we are not told that He actually visited these celebrated foreign cities. S. Paul, however, finding a Christian community in Tyre, spent a week there on the homeward voyage after his third missionary journey (Acts xxi, 3). At Sidon also he landed for a short time while on his fateful voyage to Rome (Acts xxvii, 3).

Although the history of Tyre can be traced back as far as the third millenium B.C., Sidon, the mother city, was older still. Excavation has discovered many important remains of these almost prehistoric towns, which are still seaports of some size and importance. Besieged and destroyed a hundred times, they possess natural features that Time itself can scarcely modify, and their general appearance to-day must be very much that of the New Testament times. At Tyre (*Sur*), the Mole of Alexander the Great is still visible under its deposit of sand, and part of the ancient city wall can be traced. The ancient northern or Sidonian Harbour is still in use for shipping, and preserves remains of the original quaysides, though the southern harbour has disappeared. Thirteen miles to the south of the city the great rocky promontory called the Ladder of Tyre slopes steeply to the sea as it did in the days of Christ.

Modern Sidon (*Saida*), too, is still of importance, and still used as a harbour, though scarcely living up to its first-century title of 'Mistress of Ships.' Again it is the northern harbour which survives, protected as it is by a ledge of natural rock. The ancient city extended further towards the east then than at present, and in this neighbourhood many tombs and sarcophagi of an ancient cemetery have been discovered, amongst which hundreds of the cele-brated Sidonian 'tear-bottles' of iridescent glass have been picked up.

Before we leave the " coasts of Tyre and Sidon," it may be worth while mentioning the famous seaport of Acre a few miles to the South of the former city. Acre, the Old Testament Acco, was called Ptolemais in the first century of our era. S. Paul and his companion, the Beloved Physician, touched here on their last voyage to Jerusalem, and spent a day with the disciples whom they found there. (Acts xxi,7). No first-century remains have been found, and the ancient harbour is now choked with sand, having been superseded by Haifa on the further side of the bay.

But the abiding interest of Acre is in its connection with the Crusaders, who captured it in 1104 A.D., and made it their chief seaport and headquarters in the Holy Land for nearly two hundred years. Even after its capture by the Saracens, it remained for centuries the usual landing-place of pilgrims from Europe.

That the Crusaders were sometimes curiously mistaken in their identification of the sacred sites of Palestine, will be realized from the fact that they even confounded the Sea of Galilee with the Bay of Acre, and located on the shores of the Mediterranean some of the places mentioned in the New Testament as near Tiberias ! Thus they readily assumed a connection between the name of Haifa (then called Caipha) with Cephas, the Greek name of Simon Peter, and showed the very rock in the Bay from which the Apostle used to fish ! It was traditions like these which led Robinson, the first scientific explorers of Palestine, to jettison all mediæval traditions as guides to truth.

* * * * *

Such are some of the sacred sites of Palestine. Remains which are demonstrably authentic are, as we have said, not numerous. This holy but unhappy country has always been the cockpit of the nations as it is to this day ; the

Plate V

DOORWAY TO THE CHURCH OF BETHLEHEM
Only little children may enter without stooping
(*See page* 78)

THE SYNAGOGUE AT CAPERNAUM
Here Jesus may have preached
(*See page* 84)

climate itself is hostile to the preservation of antiques ; and only too often the depredations of souvenir-hunting pilgrims have completed the work of destruction wrought by deliberate iconoclasts.

Yet a survey of the existing remains does enable us, in its cumulative effect, to visualize to some extent the Palestine of first-century Christendom.   In this way we are brought to appreciate, perhaps for the first time, the amazing detachment of Christ and His disciples.   Living in a world cluttered about with the imposing monuments of pagan supremacy, materialism, wealth, and art, the early Christians did not suffer themselves to be imposed upon, and were as little overwhelmed by Græco-Roman display as were their exiled ancestors by the marvels of Babylon.

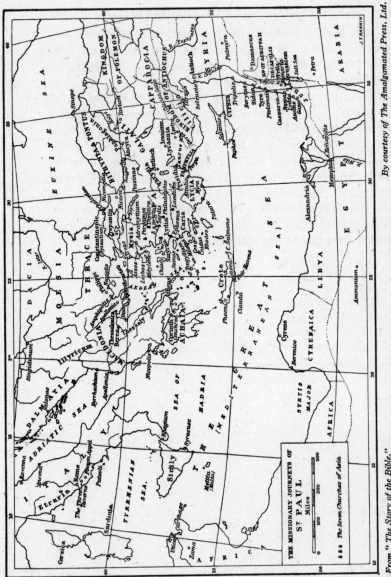

THE MISSIONARY JOURNEYS OF
St PAUL

Miles
0   100   200   300

••• The Seven Churches of Asia.

By courtesy of The Amalgamated Press, Ltd.

From " The Story of the Bible."

J.T.RANKIN

VI

ON THE TRACK OF S. PAUL

In journeyings often, in perils of waters . . . . in perils in the city, in perils in the wilderness, in perils in the sea.—
(II Corinthians xi, 26.)

AS we have walked in the footsteps of Christ and His Apostles through ' Jerusalem, and in all Judæa, and in Samaria,' so we should now follow S. Paul ' unto the uttermost part of the earth,' reconstructing from researches in Asia Minor, Greece, and Rome the environment in which he lived, and moved, and had his being.* The complete performance of so stupendous a task, however, is far beyond the compass of this volume—beyond the compass, perhaps, of any single volume. For to describe in full detail the archæological background of S. Paul and his contemporaries would entail a panoramic review of no less than the whole of the Roman Empire on its political, cultural, social, and religious side as it bestrode the civilized world in the first century of our era.

All we can attempt here is to follow S. Paul step by step along the route of his well-known missionary journeys, rebuilding out of such tumbled stones and fragments as remain the cities through which he passed, and so, perhaps, understanding his problems and his teaching a little more clearly than we did before.

* For the general subject of this chapter, read H. V. Morton : *In the Steps of S. Paul*, and all Ramsay's works.

SIR WILLIAM RAMSAY

The scientific exploration of Asia Minor came last upon the field of the Bible Lands. Not until the closing years of the nineteenth century, when Egypt, Babylonia, and Palestine had already been traversed from end to end, did it occur to anyone that the sacred sites associated with S. Paul had been almost entirely overlooked. And it is to one of our own countrymen, Sir William Ramsay, that we owe the initiative in this research.

Ramsay, like all the best scholars of his day, had been brought up to distrust the authenticity of the New Testament story of S. Paul's travels given in the Acts of the Apostles, taking it for granted that Acts was a forgery of the late second century, untrustworthy in its picture of the early Church and Empire. The only reason for this low estimate of Acts, however, had so far been of a purely literary kind, so Ramsay, winning a Research Scholarship from Oxford, thought it might be worse employed than in proving from actual observations on the field how fantastically the author of Acts had misconstrued the geographical and historical situation which he professed to describe.

It seems hard to believe that as late as the end of the nineteenth century an Alexander of Biblical scholarship should still find new worlds to conquer, but so it was. Before starting his travels Ramsay found that ' the inadequacy, the inaccuracy, and the frequent total lack of information in modern works on ancient geography, made it necessary as a first step to read afresh all the original authorities.' Among other old books on travel in Asia Minor, Ramsay turned as a last resort to the despised Acts of the Apostles. ' I began then to study the Acts in search of geographical and antiquarian evidence, hardly expecting to find any at all, but convinced that, if there were any, it would bear on the Asia Minor of the time at which the author lived, namely, about A.D. 200, and not in the least upon the first-century New Testament period.'*

But the result of Ramsay's investigation was the reverse of what he had expected. At the very outset of his journey he was made to doubt the judgment he had previously formed. On a technical point concerning the topography of Iconium, where the unanimous verdict of orthodox scholars had detected a supposed anachronism in the text, he discovered that beyond doubt the author of Acts was right after all, and the critics had been wrong. Further research brought convincing proof that in one instance after another the accuracy of Acts had been too hastily impugned, until at last Sir William Ramsay became the most enthusiastic defender of the book which he had once, so to speak, persecuted.

To his numerous works on the subject, then, we owe much of what follows in this chapter, although, of course, ' other men have entered into his labours,' and Anatolian studies have now come to the forefront, both for Old and New Testament archæological research.

For ease of reference, it will again be most convenient to deal with the discoveries in alphabetical order.

ANCYRA

Ancyra (modern Angora, or *Ankara*) was the capital of the country of Old Galatia. It is not mentioned by name in the New Testament, but those who hold the so-called ' North-Galatian Theory ' of S. Paul's first Missionary Journey believe that he must have visited it. The ruins

* W. Ramsay : *Bearing of Recent Discovery on the Trustworthiness of the New Testament* (Introduction).

of a magnificent marble Temple built by the Emperor
Augustus have always been the admiration of travellers,
and a long inscription still surviving on its walls has great
interest for New Testament studies. For an account of
this so-called *Monumentum Ancyranum*, see our chapter
on the Inscriptions (page 138f). Another interesting inscription contains a list of the Kings and Tetrarchs of Galatia,
with names of Gallic or even Gothic form.

PISIDIAN ANTIOCH

But when they departed from Perga, they came to Antioch
in Pisidia, and went into the synagogue on the Sabbath Day,
and sat down.—(Acts xiii, 14.)

' Pisidian Antioch ' (as the best manuscripts call it) is
closely associated with S. Paul, for it was here that he made
his first big effort to unite the Jewish and Gentile world
together in the new Faith. Expelled hence by the ' devout
and honourable women,' he nevertheless revisited the city
several times, and it was amongst the churches addressed
in his Epistle to the Galatians.

' The situation of Pisidian Antioch (modern *Yalovach*) is
very fine, but the locality is now deserted, forlorn, and
devoid of ruins that possess any interest or beauty.'* On
the plateau overlooking the River Anthios are the scanty
remains of the only Hellenic building of any consequence,
its massive lower-wall courses having proved too much for
the local builders to remove. A few well-preserved arches
remain of the aqueduct which conducted water to the city.
To the north-east of the site a remarkable series of rock-
cuttings as though to receive the ends of floor or roof
beams, are still visible in a natural amphitheatre of the

* W. Ramsay : *The Cities of S. Paul.*

cliffs. These are the remains of the principal Temple of
Antioch erected in honour of the god Men, the vestibule
of which perhaps survives in a few broken columns, cornices,
and other fragments.

Excavations on the site of the Temple of Men by Ramsay
just before the War discovered a colossal altar, sixty-six by
forty-one feet in size, the sanctuary being surrounded by a
wall five feet thick. The underlying soil was full of the
bones of sacrificed animals, and many engraved tablets
and emblems connected with Men were discovered. There
can be no doubt that this temple was used from the first
century onwards as a centre of the celebrated Phrygian
Mysteries which, in their observance of sacramental forms,
are believed by some to have had a certain influence on the
rites of the Christian Church.* Ramsay was able to locate
the throne of the god, and also the very spot in the centre
of the temple where worshippers were initiated into the
' New Life.' Nearby were found also three legs which
once supported the ' holy bed ' used by the god Men and
his divine spouse Demeter in their mystic nuptials.

But the most popular deity in Antioch, indeed throughout
first-century Asia Minor, was Cybele, the Great Mother
of All, identified with Diana (Artemis) and represented
usually in a simple flowing robe with two lions by her side.
For centuries before the Christian era a cave near Antioch
was venerated as sacred to the Great Mother, and is now
held sacred to the memory of the Holy Mother of God.
It has been suggested that the worship of Cybele influenced
the development of Christian veneration of the Blessed
Virgin. If this is so, it is not the only instance of a germ
of truth planted in pagan soil and brought to flower in
the sunshine of Christianity.

* S. Angus : *The Mystery Religions and Christianity* (1925).

The inscriptions found at or near Antioch are remarkably numerous, many of them having an importance for New Testament studies. Hebrew names on epitaphs written in Greek (*Debora* amongst them) prove both the existence of a large Jewish colony and also the permeation of this colony by Hellenistic influences. Intermarriage between Jew and Gentile was common, and the inter-relationship of the two races may have suggested to S. Paul a still closer union within the ' One Faith, One Baptism ' of the Christian Church. Among first-century inscriptions, one of the earliest is that of a certain P. Anicius Maximus, an officer of the Emperor Claudius (A.D. 41–54), who may have been a personal acquaintance of S. Paul's, and who served with distinction in Britain in A.D. 44.

Important in connection with the vexed question of the boundaries of New Testament ' Galatia ' is a group of Roman milestones found in the neighbourhood. These prove that the whole region of Antioch, though still included in the older geographical district known as Phrygia, belonged for administrative purposes to the Province of Galatia during the first and second centuries of our era. It was only much later (A.D. 295) that Diocletian brought it within the Province of Pisidia. Politically, therefore, Antioch was not, strictly speaking, in Pisidia at all, but in Galatia, and was therefore (as we have said) one of the churches addressed in S. Paul's Epistle to the Galatians. The monuments show that the inhabitants preferred to emphasize their up-to-date Hellenic character, rather than their connection with the barbarous Phrygians around them, and would therefore appreciate S. Paul's addressing them as ' Galatians.'

The important Antiochene inscriptions referring to Quirinius and to Sergius Paullus will be discussed in the next chapter (see page 142).

ANTIOCH IN SYRIA

The disciples were called Christians first in Antioch.—
(Acts xi, 26.)

Antioch in Syria had the honour of being both the
birthplace of the name 'Christian,' and the headquarters
of the first 'Foreign Missions' of the infant Church.
From this city S. Paul and S. Barnabas and others set
forth on those early Missionary journeys which were soon
to carry the Gospel 'unto the uttermost part of the earth.'
At Antioch was raised the first large-scale relief fund—in
aid of famine-stricken Jerusalem. And here was mooted
the great principle of freedom from the old Mosaic Law
which, adopted by the Council of Jerusalem, opened up so
wide a door for the future of Christendom. So that one
approaches Antioch in Syria as a city second only to
Jerusalem itself in importance for Christian origins. From
the general historic point of view, too, Antioch should be
full of interest to the archæologist, for it was in its day
one of the biggest and most magnificent cities of the Near
East, Capital of Syria, 'Queen of the East,' and the 'Third
Metropolis' of the Empire, furnished with everything
which Roman wealth, Greek culture, and Oriental luxury
could supply.

But alas ! modern Antioch in Syria (*Antakiyeh*) preserves
almost nothing either of its sanctity or of its splendour,
save, of course, in the natural beauty of its situation in
the lush valley of the lower Orontes with its overhanging
mountain range. Many earthquakes have shattered such
remains as escaped the hand of man. Some massive
courses of the ancient wall survive on the hill slopes, at
places eleven feet in width, and forty feet in height. At
intervals of fifty yards ruins of the protecting towers can

still be seen, with the flight of steps ascending them. Some imposing arches of Trajan's celebrated aqueduct still cross the valley, together with a well-preserved gateway or two. There are also vestiges of a great amphitheatre with its tiers of seats, and a stadium or racecourse, also with the spectators' galleries partly preserved. All this must have been very familiar to S. Paul and his friends, as must have been the remarkable rock relief, fourteen feet high, representing a female bust with headdress carved by order of that abomination of all true Jews, the wicked Antiochus Epiphanes.

There are no well-authenticated traces of the first-century Christian Church in the shabby little town of to-day, though, of course, some sacred spots are pointed out, such as the ' Cave of S. Peter,' where the earliest Christians are said to have met for worship. The so-called ' Great Chalice of Antioch ' found near this site has been described elsewhere (see page 25f).

ASSOS

And we went before to ship, and sailed unto Assos, there intending to take in Paul ; for so had he appointed, minding himself to go afoot. And when he met with us at Assos, we took him in.—(Acts xx, 13.)

Assos, modern *Bekhram*, where S. Luke picked up the Apostle on his Third Missionary Journey, stands on the crest of a hill overlooking the Ægean Sea. Excavation has revealed traces of the ancient Acropolis, surmounted by a Temple of Athena, goddess of Wisdom, and of the ancient harbour from which S. Paul set sail. The market-place (Agora) is the most complete and interesting known to archæology. Under an early Christian Church were found the remains of a first-century Roman bath, which was in existence at the time of S. Paul's visit. An inscription executed shortly before that time preserves a good example of the then current religious phraseology, so curiously like a blasphemous parody of our own Christian way of speaking—*We swear by Cæsar Augustus, our Saviour and our God, and by the Pure Virgin* [meaning the goddess Athena], *whom our fathers worshipped, that we will be faithful to Caius Cæsar Augustus* [Caligula] *and all his House.*

ATHENS

Now while Paul waited for them at Athens, his spirit was stirred in him, when he saw the city wholly given to idolatry. . . . And they took him, and brought him unto Areopagus, saying, May we know what this new doctrine, whereof thou speakest, is ?—(Acts xvii, 16f.)

The story of S. Paul's preaching in Athens on his Second Missionary Journey shows us the great Apostle face to face with the world's most skilful dialecticians, the Stoics and Epicureans of Greece, and gives us a thumbnail sketch of his impression of the city and its citizens.

A personal visit to modern Athens enables us to fill in with much vivid detail the outline of that sketch, for here is one of the few cities of antiquity whose modern appearance gives some idea of its ancient character. Hundreds of its artistic treasures, however, have been removed to the museums and public places of other and wealthier cities, our own especial perquisite being the famous Elgin marbles from the Parthenon. They are now in the British Museum, where it is possible, therefore, to delight our eyes with an example of Athenian sculpture upon which S. Paul himself must often have looked.

Most of first-century Athens has been excavated within the last two generations. Yonder is the Theatre of Dionysius, holding thirty thousand people ; here the great Stadium, where S. Paul may have witnessed those Greek Games to which he so often refers. S. Luke, the beloved Physician, may have been interested in this Temple of Æsculapius, god of Medicine, over which a Christian Church was built at a later time. An unexpected reminder of one of the darkest pages in Jewish history was the Temple of Olympian Zeus, largely built by that arch-persecutor of Judaism, Antiochus Epiphanes.

Particularly interesting to the New Testament student are the remains of the Areopagus or Mars' Hill, from which S. Paul addressed his audience on the text of the ' Unknown God.' The rock benches upon which his hearers must have sat still survive, and also the platform where the defendant was placed. In full view of this meeting-place was, and is, the famous Acropolis with its incomparable Parthenon, and the Theseum which still stands almost intact, the best preserved antiquity, it has been said, of the Greek world. A stone altar with the inscription *To the Unknown Gods* has actually been found—not at Athens, however, but at Pergamum—and a similar altar on the Palatine Hill near Rome, with the dedication *Sacred to a God or Goddess* (Plate VII). Evidently S. Paul was basing his text on a practice not unusual in the pagan world.

Visualizing thus the ' Violet-Crowned City ' of New Testament times, one marvels at S. Paul, a man so ' small and of no reputation,' braving the supercilious smiles of far-famed Athens, with these overwhelming witnesses of its undoubted achievements pressing upon him from every side. ' In the midst of these glories of architecture, only just revealed to us, and with the splendid literature of

ancient Greece in our memories, it stirs our hearts to see
S. Paul lifting up his hands, pricked and roughened with
his daily toil, before these representatives of the best
learning on the earth ; and we rejoice in his confidence that
the new Gospel of Truth could succeed even in such
surroundings.'*

CÆSAREA

*The next day we that were of Paul's company departed,
and came unto Cæsarea.*—(Acts xxi, 8.)

Cæsarea, the home of Philip the Deacon, the scene of
Peter's baptism of Cornelius, and the prison for two years
of S. Paul, is still named *Kaisariyeh*, on the sea-coast south
of Haifa.   This once magnificent seaport, founded on the
site of Strato's Tower by Herod the Great, became in New
Testament times one of the most important cities in
Palestine, the residence of the Roman procurator.   Of its
former grandeur, however, scarcely a vestige remains.
The natural pier enlarged by Herod still exists, and blocks
of granite used by him in forming the quay may be seen
under water.   Only the foundations of the ancient Temple
are now extant.   To the south of the present site lie the
chief remains of the Roman town, where the ruins of a
semi-circular theatre, which could be flooded with sea-water
for nautical spectacles, are still pointed out.   A little to
the north of this are the remains of Herod's enormous
hippodrome, built to hold twenty thousand spectators, an
obelisk, and three winning-posts of red granite still in
position.

* C. M. Cobern : *New Archæological Discoveries*, p. 491.

CORINTH

*After these things Paul departed from Athens, and came
to Corinth.*—(Acts xviii, 1.)

The beautiful but licentious city of Corinth, capital of
Roman Achæa, must have been particularly well known to
S. Paul, for he lived there on one occasion for eighteen
months at a stretch, and visited it many times. It was
while he was in Corinth that Gallio arrived (A.D. 52) as
proconsul of Achæa, but refused to interfere between S. Paul
and his enemies. To the Church in Corinth S. Paul wrote
perhaps the most human and interesting of his Epistles,
giving us a wonderfully intimate knowledge of this Paris
of the first-century world.

The site of ancient Corinth lies at a distance of about
three miles from the modern town. It still preserves
enough of its former grandeur to impress the traveller, and
many features which must have been well known to S. Paul
still in part survive. One can distinguish short stretches
of the ship-way across the isthmus, over which vessels
were hauled in those days. The Theatre, with its many
tiers of seats, has been excavated, and the famous fountain
of Pirene so well preserved that its main water-conduit is
still in use. Another celebrated fountain, the Glaucé, with
its marble lion-headed spouts, can still be seen. The
Agora, or Market Place, where S. Paul probably addressed
the jostling, pleasure-seeking crowds, has been cleared,
with its magnificent gateway and a fine series of marble
statues—which, however, were probably of a later date.
Surrounded by dark cypresses, seven gigantic Doric columns
hint at the former magnificence of the ancient Temple of
Apollo, while over it looms the abrupt rocky eminence of
Acro-Corinth nearly two thousand feet high, where the

Temple of Aphrodite sheltered the most corrupt ' religious orgies in the Empire.

The articles of furniture, ornaments, pottery, tools, etc., discovered during excavations just before the War were so numerous that a special museum had to be built to house them. Among the rather scanty inscriptions is a first-century record concerning one *Titus, a man of most noble character*, but probably not the Titus of the New Testament. An ancient door lintel was discovered bearing the sign *Synagogue of the Hebrews*, of which Deissmann says, ' It is a possibility seriously to be reckoned with that we have here the inscription to the door of the Corinthian Synagogue mentioned in Acts xviii, 4, in which S. Paul preached.' The poor, cheap workmanship of this lintel, he adds, may well illustrate the low social position of S. Paul's first converts in the city.* Concerning the proconsul of Achæa mentioned in Acts, an inscription preserving a letter of the Emperor Claudius was found at Delphi in 1905 showing that Gallio entered upon his office in the summer of A.D. 51/52, thus enabling us to fix a date for S. Paul's visit to the city.†

CRETE

When we had sailed slowly many days . . . we sailed under Crete, over against Salmone ; And hardly passing it, came unto a place which is called The Fair Havens ; nigh whereunto was the city of Lasea.—(Acts xxvii, 7.)

The island of Crete, at which S. Paul touched on his last eventful voyage to Rome, and where S. Titus became first bishop, is better known for its prehistoric ruins than for any first-century remains. Excavations at Knossos have

* A. Deissmann : *Light from the Ancient East*, p. 16.
† A. Deissmann : *Paul*, p. 261.

recovered the fabled Palace of Minos, and his royal throne, the Palace having been erected about the time of Abraham (2000 B.C.) and destroyed in the year that Joshua took Jericho (1400 B.C.). It is in a cutting of the hillside to which visitors ascended by ' the most magnificent ancient staircase in the world,' five flights of which are still in position. The celebrated Dictæan and Idæan Caves, which were still used for religious purposes in S. Paul's day, have been explored.

The jagged cliffs of Crete's inhospitable coastline, their crevices filled with snow until late in the year, still present a lee-shore perilous to sailing boats. Local tradition and a little church bearing his name fixes the site of S. Paul's landing on the north-east coast of the island.

CYPRUS

So they . . . sailed to Cyprus. And when they were at Salamis, they preached the word of God. . . . And when they had gone through the isle unto Paphos, they found a certain sorcerer, a false prophet, a Jew, whose name was Bar-jesus, which was with the deputy of the country, Sergius Paulus, a prudent man.—(Acts xiii, 4f.)

The island of Cyprus was the first overseas mission field explored by S. Paul, S. Barnabas, and the evangelist S. Mark. Here was made the first notable Roman convert to the Faith, Sergius Paulus, and here Saul changed his name to Paul, perhaps as a challenge to the Roman world.

Inscriptions throwing light upon the conversion of Sergius Paulus will be discussed below (p. 142f). To these we may add an inscription on a marble block found at Paphos. A certain Apollonius consecrates a monument to his father and mother *in the year* 13 (i.e., A.D. 55), and

Plate VI

ROMAN ARCH AT DAMASCUS
S. Paul once passed this way
(*See page* 120)

PYRAMID OF CESTIUS, ROME
S. Paul may have seen this on his way to death
(*See page* 128)

mentions that he *revised the Senate by means of assessors in
the time of the Proconsul Paulus*.   Incidentaliy, the spelling
of the name in Cyprus seems to have been with a single ' L,'
as S. Luke has it, and not with a double ' L ' as in the in-
inscriptions of Asia Minor.*

The most extensive ancient remains on the island have
been found at Salamis, which was its commercial centre in
the first century.   A large forum (market-place) has been
cleared of sand, revealing many Corinthian column-bases,
traces of a Temple of Olympian Zeus, and a large roofed
water tank approached by five arches.   The public baths
of the Roman city can be identified, as well as a typical
domestic bathroom with heating apparatus well preserved.
Near the old harbour, where S. Paul landed, is an ancient
double cistern hewn in the rock, which was converted by
the early Christians into a Church dedicated to S. Barnabas.
The walls are covered with Byzantine paintings, including a
medallion of Christ.†

There are few other remains of Roman days, though the
granite columns, known as ' S. Paul's Pillars,' were certainly
standing in S. Paul's day, being relics of a first-century
temple.

DAMASCUS

*Then was Saul certain days with the disciples which were
at Damascus.*—(Acts ix, 19.)

It was on the way to Damascus that Saul saw the heavenly
vision which converted him to Christianity.   Here, in a
house in the Street called Straight, he was baptized by
S. Ananias, and from this city he escaped the fury of the
Jews by being let down from the wall in a basket.

* C. M. Cobern : *The New Archæological Discoveries*, p 552.
† G. Jeffery : *The Ruins of Salamis* (1936).

I

Damascus (*Dimishk*) is probably the oldest continuously inhabited city in the world, a fact which is in itself detrimental to the preservation of ancient remains. The Street called Straight probably follows the ancient route, though it bears little resemblance to the Roman causeway, a mile in length and a hundred feet wide, of ancient times. First-century Damascus now lies, in fact, many feet below the surface of the modern town. There can thus be little foundation for such traditions as ' S. Paul's Tower,' whence he was let down in the basket, or the ' House of S. Ananias,' or the ' Gate of S. Thomas.'

Some Roman column bases, however, remain along the Street called Straight, now the ' Long Bazaar,' and parts of the old Roman city wall. An undoubtedly first-century relic is the East Gate (*Bab esh-Sherki*) opening upon the famous Street, a threefold archway of Roman construction, the smaller side arches, however, being now blocked up (Plate VI). Through this very gateway S. Paul may have been led sightless into Damascus after his conversion. At the entrance to the Booksellers' Bazaar are the remains of a Roman Triumphal Arch, with six Corinthian columns supporting an ornate architrave. Christian remains of a fourth-century church are also visible within the Mosque.

Concerning Aretas IV, King of Damascus in S. Paul's day (II Corinthians xi, 32), a few Aramaic inscriptions have been discovered. He ruled over the Nabatæan Arabs from 9 B.C. to A.D. 40, and somewhere between these dates was in power at Damascus. More precise information on this point, however, is at present lacking, so that the exact date of S. Paul's conversion remains uncertain. Aretas is honourably described in more than one inscription as *The King who loves his people*.*

* *Corpus Inscriptionum Semiticarum*, pt. ii, Tom. i, fasc. ii, 209.

DERBE

*And when there was an assault made . . . to use them
despitefully, and to stone them, they were ware of it, and fled
unto Lystra and Derbe, cities of Lycaonia.*—(Acts xiv, 5.)

Derbe, within the province of Galatia, was visited by
S. Paul on his first Missionary Journey, and more than
once afterwards. The site, modern *Gudelissin*, was fixed by
Sterrett in 1885, and confirmed by Ramsay, who discovered
here a remarkable series of Roman boundary stones extending without a break for several miles, marking the division
between Derbe and Barata. There are also traces of an
imperial road, marked by milestones, connecting Derbe with
Antioch. Apart from these there are no first-century
remains. The most striking natural feature of the place is a
lofty conical peak eight thousand feet in height known as
Hadji Baba, the ' Pilgrim Father,' a name now connected
by the inhabitants with S. Paul.

EPHESUS

*It came to pass that . . . Paul, having passed through the
upper coasts, came to Ephesus.*—(Acts xix, 1.)

Ephesus, the capital of Roman Asia, and the half-way
house between east and west, became for over two years
(A.D. 52–55) the residence of S. Paul. Eventually, his
success alarming the votaries of Diana of the Ephesians, he
had to move on to Macedonia. But the city became one
of the strongholds of the first-century Christian Church,
and was the recipient of one of S. Paul's most striking
Epistles.

Ephesus is one of the few sites in Asia Minor which
have yielded spectacular results to the spade of the New
Testament archæologist. In 1869 the famous Temple of

Diana (Artemis) was discovered, under romantic circumstances, twenty feet below the present level of the ground. Many of its sculptured columns and massive blocks of marble were transported to England, where they may be seen in the Ephesus gallery of the British Museum, stones hallowed by the thought that S. Paul himself must often have looked upon them.

We can now reconstruct in great detail the ritual of Diana-worship at its heyday in the time of S. Paul, and so realize the courage of his opposition to Demetrius the silversmith and all the vested interests of the priests. The venerated Image of Diana, a meteorite of human shape which had descended on the city from the skies, has not been found, but many smaller models or statuettes, such as were manufactured by Demetrius, have come to light.

Even buried treasure has been discovered on the site. In 1904 D. G. Hogarth* broke open a solid-looking stone altar, and found within it a cache of all sorts of jewellery— necklaces, brooches, coins, and so forth—evidently an ancient ' foundation deposit.' The altar had probably been used as a base for the statue of the goddess mentioned above, for around it were found vast quantities of votive offerings of all kinds, including figurines in ivory, bronze, and terra-cotta. Many of these effigies represent Diana as a beautiful woman, with full breasts, and a sort of halo around her head.

Important discoveries were made here by Austrian archæologists just before the War. They excavated the so-called ' Tomb of S. Luke,' finding it to be a pagan edifice afterwards adapted as a Christian Church. The enormous first-century Theatre was uncovered, together with adjacent buildings used for educational purposes, one of which may

* D. G. Hogarth : *Excavations at Ephesus.*

have been the School of Tyrannus where S. Paul taught (Acts xix, 9).

Inscriptions found at Ephesus are remarkably numerous, many of them having a direct bearing upon the New Testament. Thus it is interesting to note that the ministers in the Temple were called ' elders,' or ' presbyters,' just as in the early Church. The ' Asiarchs,' ' Town-clerks,' and ' Temple-keeper,' mentioned in Acts are well known by these identical names in the inscriptions. The Temple officers were elected by an assembly called the ' Ecclesia ' or ' Church.' The cry, ' Great is Diana of the Ephesians ' was a common formula in popular devotions.

There are also many references to the Magicians, whose business suffered so severely through the opposition of S. Paul (Acts xix, 19). The very oldest inscription of all, in fact, inscribed on a block of marble, describes a magical divination of omens : *If the bird is flying from right to left, then whether it rises or settles out of sight, it is unlucky*, etc.*
There is a familiar ring about this solemn nonsense ; the magicians may have burnt their books but the gibberish, horoscopes, and magic diagrams live on to delight or delude the twentieth century.

Interesting to New Testament students are the many inscriptions connected with the Greek Games from which S. Paul so often drew his imagery. The ' Golden Crown ' and ' Palm ' of victory are often mentioned. There are many references, again, to the vast business in the manufacture and sale of images of Diana. We read, for instance, that *Gaius Vibius . . . has at his own expense made a silver statue of Diana, and also two silver images, one of the city of Rome and one of the Senate, with this stipulation, that in every public assembly they shall be placed on pedestals,*

* Quoted in C. M. Cobern : *New Archæological Discoveries*, p. 474f.

for the dedication of which he has set aside to the Senate
17000 sestertia (=£170,000 !).* Needless to say, all the
' silver shrines of Diana ' mentioned in Acts xix, 24, have
long ago been purloined and melted down for their valuable
metal. The silver statue of Diana which may be seen in
the British Museum hails, not from Ephesus but from
Pergamum.

ICONIUM

It came to pass in Iconium, that they went both together into
the synagogue of the Jews.—(Acts xiv, 1.)

Iconium was visited at least four times by S. Paul, and
was one of the cities addressed in his Epistle to the Galatians.
Very few relics of first-century Iconium (modern *Konia*)
survive. The town is important, however, in the history
of New Testament criticism, because it was Sir William
Ramsay's discovery of its precise geographical position which
first converted him from his earlier distrust of Acts to a
suspicion that S. Luke might be correct.

In Acts xiv, 6, S. Luke implies that in leaving Iconium the
Apostles were crossing from the country of Phrygia into
that of Lycaonia. But Iconium, asserted the German
opponents of Acts, was itself *in* Lycaonia, therefore S. Luke
did not know what he was talking about when he represented
it as a city of Phrygia. Ramsay, however, made the discovery that although both *before* and *after* the period of
S. Paul, Iconium had indeed been assigned to Lycaonia,
yet at that particular date it was officially a city of Phrygia,
so that S. Luke turned out to be right after all. The
discovery in 1910 of two important inscriptions finally
clinched the matter by showing that as late as A.D. 150 the
inhabitants of Iconium were still using the Phrygian

* Quoted in C. M. Cobern : *New Archæological Discoveries*, p. 474f.

language on their public records, which everywhere else
were by now couched in Greek or Latin.*

LYSTRA

*There sat a certain man at Lystra, impotent in his feet. . . .
And when the people saw what Paul had done, they lifted up
their voices, saying in the speech of Lycaonia, The gods are
come down to us in the likeness of men. And they called
Barnabas, Jupiter ; and Paul, Mercurius.*—(Acts xiv, 8f.)

The site of Lystra, where S. Paul and his companion
had the unusual experience of being saluted as gods on
his first missionary journey, and which he visited at least
three times afterwards, has been identified at *Khatin Serai*,
eighteen miles south-west of Iconium.

Few traces of the first-century town have survived, but
the inscriptions are of interest. These show that, though
Lystra had been a Roman colony since A.D. 6 (many Roman
coins have been dug up), the common use of the local
vernacular, Lycaonian, persisted during the first century
and onwards, as implied in the narrative of Acts. In this
neighbourhood Ramsay also found an inscription which
showed that the Lycaonians did commonly associate Jupiter
(Zeus) and Mercury (Hermes) together in the local cult,
as S. Luke relates.†

MILETUS

*And from Miletus he sent to Ephesus, and called the elders
of the Church.*—(Acts xx, 17.)

In Miletus (modern *Palatia*) where the elders said good-
bye to S. Paul at the close of his third missionary journey,

* W. Ramsay : *Bearing of Recent Discovery*, pp. 35ff.
† ibid., pp. 48f.

'sorrowing most of all for the words which he spake, that they should see his face no more,' the ancient Temple of Apollo has been excavated, with its Sacred Way leading to the port.   There are also magnificent ruins of the Roman Theatre, with special seats inscribed *Reserved for Jews and God-fearers*.   Evidently the Jews were not everywhere as antagonistic to Hellenic spectacles as they were in Palestine.

PERGAMUM

And to the angel of the church in Pergamos write ; . . . I know thy works, and where thou dwellest, even where Satan's seat is.—(Revelation ii, 12, 13.)

We are not told that S. Paul ever visited Pergamum, but that a Christian Church existed here in the first century is witnessed in the *Revelation of S. John*.

The city has been thoroughly excavated, many splendid remains of pagan architecture, art, and religion having been found.   The frieze representing the Battle of the Giants over the great Altar of Zeus almost rivals the famous Elgin Marbles.   Sir William Ramsay thinks this altar may have been intended by the 'Satan's Seat' mentioned in Revelation, with special reference to the worship of Augustus, the Roman Emperor.

PHILIPPI

From thence to Philippi, which is the chief city of that part of Macedonia, and a colony ; and we were in that city abiding certain days.—(Acts xvi, 12.)

Philippi, the first European city to be visited by S. Paul in response to the appeal of the Man of Macedonia to 'come over and help us,' has recently been excavated.

Some ten or fifteen feet below the modern level, the ancient pavement, the very stones on which S. Paul must have walked, have been uncovered, together with the ground plan of the Market Place, and many fine buildings surrounding it. Some blocks of the old Roman Via Egnatia, connecting Philippi with its port at Neapolis, are still in position.

Coins and inscriptions corroborate S. Luke's statement that it was a ' colony.' When he says it was the ' chief city of that part of Macedonia ' it has now come to light that the word used here for ' part ' (μέρις, district) was characteristically so employed at Philippi. At one time doubt was cast upon S. Luke's accuracy in calling the governors of Philippi by the name of ' Magistrates ' (prætors), but the inscriptions prove that this title, though technically incorrect, was by courtesy allowed to the governors of a Roman colony.

PUTEOLI

We came the next day to Puteoli, where we found brethren, and were desired to tarry with them seven days.—(Acts xxviii, 13.)

At Puteoli (now *Pozzuoli*) S. Paul and S. Luke set foot at last on the *terra firma* of Italian soil after their hazardous voyage from Cæsarea.

Part of the massive mole connected with the harbour is still in existence, together with the ruins of a large Amphitheatre, Market Hall, and Temple of Augustus. In S. Paul's day Puteoli was world-famous for its merchant shipping, being the chief port of Rome, and its magnificent seafrontage must have made a deep impression on the Apostle.

ROME

When the brethren heard of us, they came to meet us as far as Appii Forum, and The Three Taverns ; whom when Paul saw, he thanked God, and took courage.   And when we came to Rome . . . Paul was suffered to dwell by himself with a soldier that kept him.—(Acts xxviii, 15.)

The story of S. Paul in Acts ends with his arrival at Rome (A.D. 61), and his two years imprisonment while awaiting the result of his appeal to Cæsar (Nero).* During these years S. Paul lived in his own hired house, writing his celebrated ' Captivity Epistles.'   At the end of this period (so it is believed) he was released for further missionary work ; only to be seized again about A.D. 64, and after a second imprisonment in Rome, put to death by order of the Emperor.

Rome, of course, has been the Eldorado of archæologists for centuries, and deserves a whole volume to itself.   All we can attempt here is the briefest sketch of its first-century remains.

Several lofty arches of the Claudia aqueduct, newly constructed at the time of S. Paul's arrival in Rome, and the striking Pyramid of Caius Cestius, perhaps the last monument on which he set eyes as he passed to his execution on the Via Ostia, are still standing (Plate. VI).   The wide expanse of the Forum (Market Place) is littered with ancient remains—three columns of the original Temple of Castor and Pollux, traces of the Basilica Julia, the Capitol, the Senate House, and the Via Sacra (Sacred Way), although the two dozen stately columns which once lined the latter now adorn the nave of the church commemorating S. Paul's

* For general information on this section, consult T. G. Tucker : *Life in the Roman World of Nero and S. Paul* (1910), and A. G. Mackinnon : *The Rome of S. Paul* (1930).

Tomb. The beautiful Bridge of Fabricius leading over the Tiber to the Temple of Æsculapius, god of Medicine, still stands to-day as it has stood since 62 B.C., much the same as it was when S. Luke the Beloved Physician may have crossed it out of a natural feeling of professional curiosity.

Many of the temples which emphasized in stone the tremendous forces of superstition surrounding the early Christians can still be identified—the Temple of Jupiter Stator, of Jupiter Capitolinus, and of the Pantheon with its marvellously preserved façade and colonnaded portico displaying the inscription on which S. Paul must often have looked, *Marcus Agrippa son of Lucius, built this temple in his third consulship* (27 B.C.). In their safe resting-place in the Vatican or elsewhere, several contemporary statues of the first-century Emperors, Augustus, Tiberius, Claudius, Nero, Domitian, convey a vivid impression of their personal appearance and even of their character.

Among the Temples, a special interest attaches to those of the foreign deities imported from Egypt and the Orient as rivals with Christianity for the allegiance of ancient Rome. One may still detect traces of the Temple of Cybele, focus of shameful rites ; and of the Temple of Isis, some lions and sphinxes surviving from its celebrated avenue, as well as an enormous bronze pine-cone once used as a fountain. The Temple of Serapis, too, has left remains, including the actual name *SERAPEUM* on a marble block, and several scattered obelisks.

Perhaps the most dangerous rival of Christianity was the mystery religion of Mithras, three of whose shrines remain well preserved in Rome and Ostia. At the latter place we can enter the low door into the sanctuary's dim recess, where the kneeling-stools of long-dead worshippers line the walls, and the mystic Signs of the Zodiac and curved markings on the floor denoting the ' seven heavens ' of Mithras can still be seen. In the Vatican Museum stands the most artistic relic of all, the famous group representing Mithras stabbing the sacrificial Bull, while man's friend the Dog attacks his enemies the Scorpion and the Snake.

It is impossible, of course, to identify with certainty the many sacred sites traditionally associated with S. Paul, S. Peter, or their disciples. The ' House of S. Paul ' in the Via degli Strengari is at any rate ancient, and lay in the ancient Jewish quarter of the city, where we may assume that S. Paul took up his abode. Nero's Judgement Hall, where S. Paul was tried, may well lie, as claimed, beneath the present Hall built by Domitian. Persistent tradition locates the Tomb of S. Paul at the Basilica so named on the Via Ostia, and the impressive underground dungeon (formerly entered only by a hole in the roof) in the Mamertine Prison is not unlikely to have been his last place of confinement.

One of the best authenticated sites is that of the ' House of Hermas '—the Hermas (or Hermes) saluted by S. Paul in Romans xvi, 14—now under the Church of S. Sebastian, where it is said the bodies of S. Paul and S. Peter lay for a while after their martyrdom. Recent excavation has revealed a first-century Roman house with adjacent tombs, together with very early inscriptions and wall-paintings. One of the inscriptions records that Hermas at the age of seventy-five emancipated all his slaves, possibly as a result of his conversion from paganism. The house was built about A.D. 40, and the ornamentation, at first pagan, then later Christian, is said to indicate its occupier's sudden change of religion. Some skeletons still remain in the graves, just as they were laid nineteen hundred years ago.

Another well-authenticated site is the ' House of Prisca

and Aquila,' which is proved by excavation to date from pre-Christian times. Not far away lie the remains of an old Roman bath constructed by Novatus, grandson of the above, over which his sister, S. Prassedes, built the church named after her, probably the oldest Christian church in Rome.

The stately Triumphal Arch of Titus and the imposing ruins of the Colosseum, though not erected until A.D. 81, some fifteen years after the death of S. Paul, were all too familiar spectacles to the early Church. The Arch of Titus commemorates the Fall of Jerusalem (A.D. 70) in an elaborate relief of Roman soldiers carrying aloft in procession the golden Seven-branched Candlestick, the silver Trumpets, and the Table of Shew-bread which had been looted from the Temple in Jerusalem.

Such are some of the first-century remains of New Testament Rome. It has to be remembered that the great fire of A.D. 64, inflamed by Nero, as well as many attacks on the city in the centuries that were to come, obliterated many of the landmarks familiar to S. Paul.

TARSUS

But Paul said, I am a man which am a Jew of Tarsus, a city in Cilicia, a citizen of no mean city.—(Acts xxi, 39.)

The site of Tarsus (modern *Tersous*), the capital of Cilicia where S. Paul was born, and of which he was so proud a citizen, is especially interesting for its connection with the Apostle's earliest years, although it was under Gamaliel in Jerusalem that he was chiefly educated. (Acts xxii, 3.)

Unfortunately little remains of the glory that was Tarsus. It is now no more than ' a shabby little town where rows of wooden shacks face each other across roadways of hard mud.' (H. V. Morton.) No trace has survived of the famous University of Tarsus, the marble colonnades along the embankment of the River Cydnus, or the noble public buildings which bequeathed to this once magnificent city the title, still to be seen on its coinage, of ' Loveliest, Greatest Metropolis.' Even the river has now changed its course away from the town, and the capacious harbour into which the galleons of Cleopatra once sailed is now no more than a fever-stricken marsh. Only two huge platforms of stone, the so-called ' Tomb of Sardanapalus,' in a walled enclosure overgrown with weeds, survives as an indubitable relic of New Testament times ; the ruins, probably, of a Roman temple. There is also an ancient Roman gateway bearing the name of S. Paul's Arch, which is usually attributed to Hadrian.

A little to the north of Tarsus lies the narrow pass famous in history under the name of the ' Cilician Gates,' in the solid rock of which a path had been chiselled out many centuries before the Christian era, and still remains, together with some ancient inscriptions on the cliff-side.

Ramsay has made a very full study of the coinage of Tarsus, showing that for many centuries the two forces of Hellenism and Orientalism struggled for control of the city. The Oriental outlook persisted even to the first century, and has been thought to account for S. Paul's attitude to women. Coins struck by Antiochus Epiphanes in 175–164 B.C. show that Tarsus was re-founded by him about that date as the self-governing capital of Cilicia. Henceforward its complexion became increasingly Hellenic, although there is evidence of a strong resident community of Jews. In 64 B.C. Pompey occupied and colonised the city, thus introducing the privilege of Roman citizenship, which S. Paul inherited.

THESSALONICA

They came to Thessalonica, where was a synagogue of the Jews.—(Acts xvii, 1.)

S. Paul on his second missionary journey spent three weeks at Thessalonica, only to find he had got Jason, his host, into trouble for harbouring one who ' had turned the world upside down.' The Church in this city, however, prospered, and to it S. Paul wrote two of the earliest of his letters, the Epistles to the Thessalonians.

It is doubtful whether the British forces stationed at *Salonica* during the Great War saw much in the neighbourhood to remind them of the city of S. Paul. The main street covers a stretch of the ancient Via Egnatia, but the Roman arch of Galerius is later than the New Testament era.

Inscriptions found on the site, however, have established S. Luke's accuracy in calling the magistrates of Thessalonica by the unusual name of ' Politarchs,' a title once suspect on the grounds that it occurs nowhere in Classical literature. One of these interesting inscriptions has been removed to the British Museum.

TROAS

And they passing by Mysia came down to Troas. And a vision appeared to Paul in the night ; There stood a man of Macedonia, and prayed him, saying, Come over into Macedonia, and help us.—(Acts xvi, 8.)

Alexandria Troas, where S. Paul received his well-known summons to cross over to Europe, and where he probably first met his biographer S. Luke, still preserves traces of its ancient magnificence as a favoured city of Augustus, and one of the most important seaports of western Asia.

Amongst the trees which fill the vast enclosure of its walls, are fragments of colossal masonry, with the ruins of a Greek Theatre, and mighty arches, traditionally called the ' Palace of Priam,' but probably remains of the Greek Gymnasium, still conspicuous on approaching the harbour from the sea.

That the name of Priam has been associated with this site is due to the fact that Troas was identified in ancient times with the Homeric city of Troy, which is now known, as a result of Schliemann's excavations, to have occupied the mound of *Hissarlik* a short distance away.

Such are a few of the more notable archæological discoveries which have rewarded the explorer or excavator as he followed in the footsteps of S. Paul. It must be admitted that nothing explicitly mentioning the great Apostle or any of his converts or companions has been discovered, unless we include the name of Sergius Paulus ; and few indeed of the actual stones on which he walked, or the marbles on which he looked, have survived the stress of the centuries in any recognizable form. Yet our survey of the remains has, in its cumulative effect, enabled us to reconstruct some sort of a picture of the world in which he lived, and to visualize the physical background of the scene in which the infant Church struggled towards its adolescence.

Plate VII

A ROMAN PENNY
Whose image and superscription hath it?
By permission of the Trustees of the British Museum. (*See page* 147)

WARNING : NO TRESPASSERS !
Found in the Temple at Jerusalem
(*See page* 73)

AN ALTAR TO AN UNKNOWN GOD
Similar to the one S. Paul saw in Athens
(*See page* 114)

VII

THE EVIDENCE OF THE INSCRIPTIONS

INSCRIPTIONS ON STONE, METAL, COINS, GRAFFITI, AND OSTRAKA

Whatsoever things were written aforetime were written for our learning.—(Romans xv, 4).

O F all the varied objects of antiquity which the spade has discovered or exploration brought to light, inscriptions have always ranked high in the estimation of the archæologist.* However much he may be able to deduce from the appearance of blocks of masonry, statuary, sculptured stones, ancient weapons, utensils, tools, sepulchres, and the like, it is as nothing to the explicit and often unique source of information he may find in the contemporary written records of the past.

THE VALUE OF INSCRIPTIONS

This is more particularly true of the ages before literature, as we know it, became a commonplace of existence, supplying in an easily reduplicated and transmitted form all (and sometimes more than all !) the information we desire. Thus the inscriptions of ancient Egypt, Assyria, Babylonia, and the Near East in general, are indispensable to an understanding of Old Testament history, because, apart from the Biblical record itself, they are virtually our sole source of information for the period.

* For this chapter consult A. Deissmann : *New Light from the Ancient East*, and Ramsay's works.

In the New Testament era, adequately documented as it is by the writings of the most literary peoples in antiquity, Greeks, Romans, and Jews, inscriptions naturally take a lower place. Or perhaps one should say a different, rather than a ' lower ' place, for even in New Testament archæology the inscriptions do retain an importance all their own.

In the first place, the inscriptions have this advantage over books, that they always (or nearly always) give a contemporary record of the events, and a first edition, as it were, of that record. Ordinary literature is written sometimes long afterwards, written with second-hand knowledge, and written from a tendencious point of view. Add to this, that the books of antiquity had to be copied by hand, and the copies copied again, until at length the invention of printing stereotyped for ever some fortuitously chosen and possibly defective manuscript.

Compared with this, an inscription (using the term in its widest sense) comes to us fresh from the pen of the writer. It is the actual original, the ' autograph,' reaching across the centuries in a form altered only by the impartial hand of Time. We can see the scratch of the chisel where it slipped, the blot inadvertently made by the scribe's over-loaded pen, the hesitant erasure in the text, the misspelling, the careless grammar, the unvarnished actuality, in short, of what was written down.

This is not, of course, to claim that inscriptions cannot lie. They can, and do. The Pharaohs of Egypt have more than once been ' caught out ' in falsifying their hieroglyphic inscriptions, and the cuneiform of the Assyrian Kings is not always above suspicion. But the archæologist does not mind this sort of lie for he feels—paradoxical though it may sound—that his reconstruction of the human past would not be true without a falsehood or two to fill in the picture.

Again, the inscriptions often give a glimpse into little odd corners of the past which have been completely overlooked by the literary historian. It is easy, from ordinary history books, to get the impression that life in days gone by was always on the grand scale—great kings and leaders of men, great battles lost or won, great cities built, great movements of the mind. But archæology is making us realize that it was not so in ancient times any more than it is to-day. In the first century as in the twentieth, Tom, Dick, and Harry formed by far the greatest proportion of the population of all countries, and if we would know what the world was really like, it is not into the palaces of potentates, but into the humble little homes of ordinary men and women that we must peep.

The modern man-in-the-street often leaves no personal record behind him save in an inscription—his name upon a tombstone, initials on a choirboy's seat, a private letter or two—and it was much the same in the first century, except that his letters were often written on virtually imperishable pieces of pottery, or on papyrus which the dry sand of Egypt has marvellously preserved. By scraps such as these, we have been able to build up a reconstruction of his life and times, which no literary writer could or would give us.

For the present, however, we will confine ourselves to the inscriptions proper. In the New Testament period the bulk of these were on stone, but many have been found which were cast in metal, engraved on bronze, or scratched on tablets of lead or gold, together with a few wax and wooden tablets, scribblings (*graffiti*) on walls, and the superscriptions on coins and medals. Of these there are hundreds of thousands of examples, but of course we have space to mention only a few of those most relevant to our purpose.

INSCRIPTIONS ON STONE

Some of the stone inscriptions have already been noted in the preceding chapters, usually under the heading of the locality in which they were found. The celebrated inscription found on the Temple of Augustus (see page 107) at Ancyra (*Ankara*) now demands more detailed notice.

The Monumentum Ancyranum, written in Latin and Greek, is the most complete of several versions of the same text, fragments of which have been found at Appollonia and at Antioch in Pisidia.* Composed by the Emperor Augustus towards the end of his life (A.D. 14), it gives a dignified though self-laudatory account of his work for the Empire. The imperial honours paid to him are fully recorded, and the beneficent effects of his rule. For instance, it states that the Gate of Janus which was shut only when victorious peace has been secured by land and sea, and only twice before the birth of Augustus, had been shut no less than thrice during his rule. . . . He gave frequent gratuities of corn and money, never to less than 250,000 people. He was the first to plant colonies of soldiers in conquered lands. He spent much time and money on the building of temples, aqueducts, and other public works. He gave innumerable games and shows. The frontiers of his wide Empire are detailed, its many Provinces being enumerated by name. There is, however, no special mention of Syria or Palestine, except the statement that he planted a colony of soldiers at Berytus (*Beirut*), so the inscription fails us in this respect, just where we should have been most interested.

* For this section consult E. G. Hardy : *Monumentum Ancyranum.*

NEW LIGHT ON THE NATIVITY CENSUS

The most important part of the record, for our purpose, is the account it gives of an imperial census or enrolment, thus : *I performed the census after an interval of 42 years. At this census 4,063,000 Roman citizens were entered on the rolls. A second time, in the consulship of C. Censorinus and C. Asinius, I completed a census with the help of a colleague invested with the consular imperium. At this second census 4,233,000 Roman citizens were entered on the rolls. A third time I completed a census, being invested with the consular imperium, and having my son Tiberius Cæsar as my colleague. At this third census 4,937,000 Roman citizens were entered on the rolls.*

Scholars connect the three Enrolments above-mentioned with the years 28 B.C., 8 B.C., and A.D. 14, there being an interval of about twenty years between each occasion. It is to be noted that each census is an enumeration not of population, but of Roman citizens. It is a striking thought, that among the 4,937,000 citizens of the Third (A.D. 14) Census, the name of young Saul of Tarsus, Roman citizen by right of birth (Acts xxii, 28) was probably entered on the official list.

It is with the *Second* Census (that of 8 B.C.), however, that we are most concerned. Unfortunately, apart from this mention in the *Monumentum Ancyranum*, no other allusion to this Census is extant, the records of Augustus' earlier years being very imperfect. Is this, or is it not, the Census referred to by S. Luke when he says that *It came to pass in those days that there went out a decree from Cæsar Augustus that all the world should be taxed*—the Enrolment, in fact, which caused Joseph and the Blessed Virgin to go to Bethlehem just before the Birth of the Holy Child (S. Luke ii, 4) ?

Since there is no mention of any imperial Census between
8 B.C. and A.D. 14, it would seem possible that this Second
Census of the *Ankara* monument may be the Census of
the Gospel, and that Christ must therefore have been born
about 8 B.C.

It may seem strange to suggest that Christ was born in
any year B.C., that is ' Before Christ,' but as far as that goes,
there is no difficulty, for it has long been known that
the Abbot Dionysius Exiguus, who invented the ' B.C. ' and
' A.D.' system in the sixth century, was a few years ' out ' in
his chronology.

THE GOVERNORSHIP OF QUIRINIUS

The question, however, is complicated by the fact that
S. Luke proceeds to give a *second* time-note, in addition to
the first.   In his Chapter ii, verse 1, he says the Census was
decreed by Cæsar Augustus (i.e., in 8 B.C.), but in verse 2,
he says it *was first made when Cyrenius (Quirinius) was
Governor of Syria.*

Now it is a well-known fact of history that Quirinius was
Governor of Syria in A.D. (*not* B.C.) 6, and that he ordered
a local (not, of course, an *imperial*) Census in that year.
Has S. Luke made a mistake, then, in his dates ? Has
S. Luke confused the Census of A.D. 6 with the Census of
8 B.C. ?   Hardly ; for we know, as it happens, that he could
not have done anything of the kind, since he actually
mentions this *later* Census of Quirinius in Acts, showing
that he was perfectly well aware when it took place, namely
in connection with Judas of Galilee in A.D. 6 (Acts v, 37).
The only explanation remaining is that S. Luke knew of a
previous Census taken during a Governorship of Quirinius
before the death of Herod the Great (4 B.C.).

THE LAPIS TIBURTINUS

Have we any evidence outside the Gospel that Quirinius did in fact ' govern ' Syria in B.C. as well as in A.D., or, in other words, that he became Governor *twice* ?

Unfortunately no explicit literary record exists to this effect (there are many historical gaps at this period), but there is an inscription, the celebrated *Lapis Tiburtinus** found at Rome in 1828, which may be taken into account.

An extract from this Inscription runs as follows :—

[Missing name] *Consul . . . as Proconsul obtained Crete and Cyrene as his Province. . . . As Legate of the divine Augustus, obtaining Syria and Phœnicia, he waged war with the tribe of Homonadenses who had killed Amyntas their king. When he returned into the dominion of the Emperor Cæsar Augustus and the Roman People, the Senate decreed thanksgiving to the gods for his successful campaign and triumphal ornaments to him. As Proconsul he obtained Asia as a Province. As Legate of the divine Augustus, he obtained again Syria and Phœnicia. . . .*

In the opinion of the great Roman historian Mommsen, the missing name at the beginning of this inscription can be none other than P. Sulpicius Quirinius, and it can be taken as proving that Quirinius was in authority over Syria twice, both B.C. and A.D.

According to Mommsen, this first Governorship of Syria was about 3 B.C., but Ramsay has produced evidence that it must have been some four or five years earlier, thus coinciding with the date of the Second Census of Augustus mentioned on the *Monumentum Ancyranum*.

Ramsay's evidence appears in inscriptions found at

---

* *Corpus Inscriptionum Latinarum* xiv, 3613.

Antioch in Asia Minor, which name Publius Sulpicius Quirinius as Commander-in-Chief of the Roman armies in the Homonadensian War of 10-7 B.C., with military jurisdiction over Syria. He infers, therefore, that Quirinius was in charge of the military organization of Syria in these troublous times, being freely called ' Governor ' of the country by his contemporaries, while his colleague, one Sergius Saturninus, was simultaneously in charge of the civil administration with the official title of Procurator of Syria—as we know from Tertullian and others. The pieces of this age-old puzzle therefore fall neatly into place, and once more S. Luke emerges triumphantly from the cross-examination of his critics.

According to this, Jesus was born about 8 B.C., which would make Him almost exactly thirty-two years old when His ministry began in A.D. 26. Or the Census in Judæa, owing to special circumstances connected with Herod's jurisdiction, may have been extended a few years, making His birth 5 or 6 B.C. Here, then, we find yet another confirmation of S. Luke's Gospel, which states He was ' about thirty years old ' when He began to preach (S. Luke iii, 23). We shall have more to say about the Census and S. Luke's accuracy in connection with it, when we examine the evidence of the papyri (see pages 152, 169).

SERGIUS PAULUS OF CYPRUS

Among the numerous inscriptions found by Ramsay* at Antioch of Pisidia, was one engraved on a block of stone thus : *To Lucius Sergius Paullus the younger, son of Lucius, one of the four commissioners in charge of the Roman streets, tribune of the sixth Legion, etc.* By a series of deductions too

---

* W. Ramsay : *Bearing of Recent Discovery*, p. 150ff.

technical to reproduce here, Ramsay was able to refer this inscription actually to the son of that Sergius Paullus (spelled here with two Ls) proconsul of Cyprus, who was so impressed by S. Paul's preaching at Paphos (Acts xiii, 4f). The inscription shows that the Proconsul's son successfully followed in his father's footsteps as an official of the Government.

But that was not all. Another inscription was found to shed still further light on this Sergius Paullus. It refers to a certain Gaius Caristanius Fronto, legate of the Emperor Domitian, and his wife 'the most excellent Sergia Paulla, daughter of Lucius Sergius Paullus.' Ramsay deduced from a comparison of dates and other factors that this Sergia Paulla was the daughter of the senior Lucius, Proconsul of Cyprus, and the sister of the younger Lucius, the date of her marriage to C. Caristanius Fronto being about A.D. 72.

Now Sergia Paulla had two sons, of whom we know something of the elder, Gaius Caristanius Fronto Junior. We know from various inscriptions discovered by Ramsay in Asia Minor, that he abandoned his Roman name Caristanius, that he gave up the Latin language in favour of Greek, and that he did *not* follow his father or his grandfather in accepting government office. This attitude on the part of Paulla's son can best be understood (says Ramsay) if his mother, daughter of S. Paul's namesake in Cyprus, had become a Christian and brought up her son in the same Faith, thus inevitably closing against him the doors of a political career. In other words, through the study of these at first sight irrelevant inscriptions, we have unexpectedly stumbled upon what looks remarkably like a corroboration of S. Luke's story that the Roman Proconsul of Cyprus, despite his high office, gave ear to S. Paul's preaching, *and believed, being astonished at the doctrine of the Lord* (Acts xiii, 12).

It is unlikely that he himself made open profession of his conversion, but it seems that his daughter may have done so, and that his grandson from the first may have been reared as a Christian.   The argument, it should be said, is far more forcible when studied with all that wealth of detail and erudite allusion brought to bear upon it in Ramsay's works.

THE TOMB-ROBBER'S INSCRIPTION

An interesting inscription has been found at Nazareth, known as the ' Tomb-robbers' Inscription,'* which may shed some light on the circumstances connected with our Lord's Resurrection.   A free translation runs as follows :—

By order of the Emperor.   I desire that all sepulchres and tombs which have been made out of respect to the dead, whether parents, children, or relations, shall remain undisturbed in perpetuity.   Anyone found interfering with the dead or nefariously removing coffins or headstones will be prosecuted as an offender against divine and human law, for great respect should be paid to the dead, and no one may lawfully disturb them. Anyone found guilty of such a crime shall be liable to capital punishment as a Tomb-robber.

The inscription is written in Greek, though apparently translated from a Latin original, and has been dated at the beginning of the Christian era, possibly about A.D. 10.   If this is the case, it must have been well known to Pontius Pilate when he arranged to have the sepulchre of Jesus guarded against depredation (S. Matthew xxviii, 11-15), and perhaps to the Apostles as they stood bewildered before the Empty Tomb at that first Eastertide.

* *P.E.F.Q.*, 1932, p. 85 (S. A. Cook).

THE SYNAGOGUE INSCRIPTION OF THEODOTUS

Amongst other interesting inscriptions one found by Weill in Jerusalem just before the War may be mentioned. It is written in Greek on a slab of stone at a date most probably within the New Testament period, and gives us an exceedingly vivid glimpse of the religious life of the Holy City as the central resort of Jewish pilgrims from all over the world—such as those who gathered at Pentecost.

This ' Synagogue Inscription of Theodotus ' runs as follows : *Theodotus, son of Vettenus, priest and ruler of the synagogue, son of a ruler of the synagogue, built this synagogue for reading of the Law and for teaching of the Commandments. Also the stranger's lodging and apartments, and the conveniences of waters for an inn for them that need it from abroad, of which Synagogue his fathers and the Elders and Simonides did lay the foundation.*

It has been suggested that here we have a relic of the synagogue of the Libertines mentioned in Acts vi, 9. It throws at any rate an interesting light on the manifold activities connected with a synagogue.

THE TENTH LEGION VETERAN'S INSCRIPTION

Another exceedingly interesting inscription is one that was discovered in the Fayyum in Lower Egypt in 1909, written on a folding pair of wooden tablets in Latin, with reference to one Marcus Valerius Quadratus, a veteran of the Tenth (Fretensian) Legion which, under the command of Titus, destroyed Jerusalem in A.D. 70.* The date of the inscription is A.D. 94, and it records certain privileges, awarded by the Emperor Domitian to his ex-service men. *You are to be exempt from all taxes ; you and your wife and*

* A. Deissmann : *New Light from Ancient East*, p. 442ff.

*children shall be Roman Citizens with all rights thereof.
This applies to all who have served at Jerusalem in the Tenth
Fretensian Legion, and have been discharged with an honourable
discharge, having served full time.*

The tablet professes to be a copy of an inscription in brass
which had been set up in the Great Cæsareum at Alexandria,
and evidently served as a kind of receipt for exemption
whenever the old campaigner was approached for his
income tax. An inscribed boundary-stone of the camp
occupied by this famous Legion is still in existence in
Jerusalem, as well as several tiles marked with the Legion's
initials.

COINS OF PALESTINE

Numismatology, the science of coins, is a big word, and
it is a big subject, for a discussion of all the coins which
were in use within the Roman Empire during New Testament times would take us very far afield.   Nevertheless, we
must not entirely overlook these tiniest inscriptions of all,
even though we confine ourselves to the coinage of first-
century Palestine.*

In our Lord's day three metals were used for money—
gold, silver, and copper (brass)—an allusion to this being
made in the Gospel, *Get you no gold, nor silver, nor brass
in your purses* (S. Matthew x, 9 R.V.).   In later days, the
golden standard coin (equivalent to our pound) was called
Libra ; the silver coinage, Solidi ; the copper, Denarius ;
or all together as L.S.D., initials which we all understand.

A.   Of *SILVER* coins in New Testament times there are
several named in the Gospels.

(1) The *Denarius*, translated ' Penny ' in our versions, but
in the American Bible ' Shilling,' which is nearer the mark.

* Consult, British Museum : *Guide to Roman Coins* (1927) ; *Coins of Palestine* (1914).

Many examples of the Roman Penny survive to lend point to the well-known words : *Show Me the tribute money. And they brought unto Him a Penny.* *And He saith unto them, Whose is this image and superscription? They say unto Him, Cæsar's. Then saith He unto them, Render therefore unto Cæsar the things which are Cæsar's ; and unto God the things that are God's.* (S. Matthew xxii, 19).

How very much more real the incident becomes when we hold in our hand an actual Denarius such as He must have held in His ! It is of silver, unmilled, that is, without the serrated edge familiar in modern coins, and rather smaller than a modern shilling. On the obverse is stamped the ' image ' or portrait of the Roman Emperor, with the ' superscription ' *TI[BERIUS] CÆSAR DIVI AUG[USTI] F[ILIUS] AUGUSTUS.* (*Tiberius Cæsar Augustus, son of the divine Augustus.*) On the reverse is the superscription *PONTIF[EX] MAX[IMUS]* (*High Priest in Rome*) with an image of the Empress *LIVIA*, seated, in her right hand a sceptre, in her left a flower (Plate VII).

(2) *The Drachma*, translated in S. Luke xv, 8, ' pieces of silver,' was another coin of similar value but based on the Greek (Attic) standard, which ran concurrently with the Roman.

(3) *The Didrachma*, translated ' half-shekel ' in S. Matthew xvii, 24 (R.V.), was twice the value of the above, and was the due payable by every Jew for the support of his Temple.

(4) *The Stater* or Tetradrachm of Antioch, translated ' skekel ' in S. Matthew xvii, 27 (R.V.), was equivalent to a Jewish shekel. It shows the head of the Emperor, with a figure of Victory on the reverse.

B. Among *COPPER* coins, we read in the New Testament of the following :—

(1) *The Lepton*, translated in S. Mark xii, 42 as ' mite '

(the widow's mite) was the smallest coin in Palestine, half the size of a Victorian threepenny bit.

(2) *The Quadrans*, translated ' farthing ' in the same passage, was twice the value of a Lepton.

(3) *The Assarion*, also translated as ' farthing ' in S. Matthew x, 29. Of this coin we have a specimen actually struck by Pontius Pilate in the year of the Crucifixion (A.D. 29), the sixteenth of Tiberius. On the obverse is the superscription in Greek TIBEPIOY KAIΣAPOY (*of Tiberius Cæsar*), with the image of the Sacrificial Ladle and three Ears of Corn bound together. On the reverse is the name of *JULIA*, mother of the Emperor.

Such are a few of the coins which were in circulation in Palestine during the first century and of which many examples survive. The whole question is complicated by the fact that several different currencies were simultaneously in vogue, namely coins from Persian, Greek, Syrian, and Roman mints, hence the importance of the ' money-changers ' of whom we read in the Gospels (S. Mark xi, 15).

It should be noted that the Herodian princes from 37 B.C.-A.D. 100, coined bronze money bearing their names (Herod, Herod Agrippa I, or Herod Agrippa II) in Greek, thus BAΣIΛEYΣ HPΩΔOY (*King Herod*), together with the year of his reign and the usual three Ears of Corn. Also, during the revolt of the Jews A.D. 68-70, the issue of Jewish money was revived in Jerusalem, shekels and half-shekels of silver bearing the names *ELEAZAR* or *SIMON*, being struck.

Of special interest to Bible readers is a large bronze coin or medal, rather heavier than a modern penny, struck by the Emperor Titus to commemorate the destruction of Jerusalem in A.D. 70. On the obverse is a bust of the Emperor with his titles, and on the reverse, the picture of a fully-armed Roman soldier standing on guard over a Jewish woman captive, who sits weeping under a palm tree. The inscription runs *JUDÆA CAPTA S.C.* (*Judæa taken captive by order of the Senate*).

Specimens of most of the coins used throughout the Empire in the first century have been found, and may be examined in our museums. Some of them are of special interest as preserving delineations of architectural and other remains now lost or in ruins. The coins of Ephesus, for example, show the ancient Temple of Diana of the Ephesians, her statue within the portico. The highly ornamented column-bases of this portico thereon depicted can be compared with actual originals of those bases now in the British Museum.

WALL SCRIBBLINGS OR GRAFFITI

The wall-scribblings and rough scrawls (they hardly merit the name inscription) left by the idle or semi-literate passer-by of ancient times, add little to our information as to the history of the period, yet they have an interest of their own. One sympathizes with the exasperation of the labourer, who, compelled, perhaps, to work overtime on the building of the palace of Simon Maccabæus, scrawled on its walls : *To Blazes with Simon's palace ! says Pampras.*

There is something very intimate, too, in the rough marks on some builders' stones in Jerusalem, *Bad work*, or *Cover this up*. One of the very oldest inscriptions in the world, found on a Jar in the prehistoric strata at Lachish, has been deciphered with much laborious ingenuity as *This side up*.

Coming to our own period, there is the celebrated but blasphemous caricature of Christ represented with the head of an ass looking down from the Cross upon a young man who salutes Him with uplifted hand. The inscription runs (we attempt to reproduce the faulty spelling) *Alexamenos adors 'is God.* (Αλεξαμενος σεβε τε θεων.) Some of the *graffiti* are not only blasphemous, but indecent, as is the way in all ages.

And many of them, of course, are the amatory effusions of eternally love-sick youth, such as : *I am in love with Harmonia. The number of her darling name is* 45. He meant that her name consisted of the numbers 1, 2, 3, 4, 5, 6, 7, 8, 9 (= 45) which make a perfect sequence, and signify that the lady herself was Perfect. This punning, as it were, with numbers was a common practice, and is exemplified even in the New Testament where the number 666 (or 616) numerical equivalent of Nero, is described as ' the mark of the Beast ' (Revelation xiii, 17, 18). Among typical amatory *graffiti*, are *My blonde has made me hate brunettes—Brunettes for me, I always did like blackberries !—Restitutus is a flirt !— I'll give anything to a pretty girl, but no common one need apply—Miss Snub-nose looks pretty to me.*

The *graffiti* are of all kinds, as is well seen on the walls of Pompeii so wonderfully preserved by their long burial in volcanic ash. There is a rough head of Nero, with his name scrawled below it—a very necessary aid to identification ! Political slogans are common : *Vote for Publius Furius as duumvir ; he is a good man.—Vote for Fuscanus as alderman !* and so on. Showing the strong belief of the poorer classes, even among non-Christians, in the Life of the world to come, are several *graffiti* addressed to the dead : *Thou art dead, beloved ; cheer up, I shall soon be with thee !* Many of the remarks are just rude—*Sodom and Gomorrah !* wrote someone on a house in Pompeii ; and on a wall : *Samnius to Cornelius : Go and hang yourself !*

Insignificant though these scribblings may be from the

Plate VIII

A TYPICAL LETTER OF NEW TESTAMENT TIMES
Written in Greek on papyrus
By permission of the Trustees of the British Museum. (See page 157)

THE OLDEST NEW TESTAMENT MANUSCRIPT IN EXISTENCE
A fragment of S. John's Gospel, A.D. 140
(See page 176)

point of view of literature, art, or the major issues of ancient history, they do undoubtedly help us to realize how human, how very much of the same flesh and blood as we are to-day, were the ordinary folk amongst whom the Gospel was preached in the period of the New Testament.

POTSHERDS OR OSTRAKA

A grade higher than the *graffiti*, but still chiefly used only by the very poor, or else for very humble purposes, were the inscribed potsherds (*ostraka*) or broken pieces of earthenware, which have been turned up in such large numbers all over the ancient East. In the early days of research they were thrown aside with scarcely a glance, but to-day they are like ' the stone which the builders rejected,' for they have oftentimes become ' the head of the corner ' of some important piece of archæological reconstruction. In Old Testament studies, for instance, the *ostraka* of Samaria, and the recently discovered *ostraka* of Lachish, rank amongst the most notable discoveries of our time.*

Inscribed potsherds of the New Testament era, chiefly written in Greek, have survived in considerable numbers, and are particularly valuable for the light thrown upon the ordinary daily life, ' the trivial round and common task,' of the poor, the very folk, in fact, amongst whom the Gospel made its earliest converts. Too poverty-stricken to buy papyrus, still less parchment, these early Christians and their neighbours resorted to broken fragments of domestic pottery, whereon to write their letters, household accounts, receipts, recipes, labels, and even documents for more important and permanent use, such as their prayer books and portions of Holy Writ.

* S. L. Caiger : *Bible and Spade*, p. 193f.

K

A begging letter written to a clergyman of the early church shows how little human nature or human methods have changed. *First I greet thee, devout and reverend gentleman ; may God bless thee and thine ! Please be generous, and have pity upon this poor man !* Another letter to a priest is most pathetic : *Please pray for me. Didst thou know the plight I am in, thou wouldst be grieved indeed. I have never been in greater trouble. If I can find two loaves, even one loaf, a day, my children and I will not die.* In another a parishoner expresses surprise that his pastor has not visited him in his sickness. Another ends : *Please excuse me for not being able to find a piece of papyrus to write on, as I am in the country.*

With reference again to S. Luke's Census (S. Luke ii, 1), considerable interest attaches to the many census-dockets which have been found inscribed on papyrus or *ostraka* of various kinds, dating from the first and immediately subsequent centuries. It is probable that the questionnaire may have become more or less stereotyped, as is the habit of official documents, and therefore that the enrolment return of S. Joseph might have appeared in somewhat the following form, which is frequently exhibited : *In the . . . year of the Emperor . . .* (the imperial titles here follow), *I . . . son of . . . aged . . . years, with a . . . nose, . . . hair, and* (here follow any special identification marks), *enroll myself : Together with . . . my wife, aged . . . years.* (Here follows the signatory's name, and a statement of his property, so many camels, sheep, etc., and the address at which he normally lives.)

Many first-century census-returns of this description have been discovered relating to Jewish citizens. Amongst the names recorded on them are *Didymus, Jesus, Theophilus,* and others familiar in the nomenclature of the New Testament.

One of the most remarkable discoveries among the *ostraka* was a portion of the New Testament written on a consecutively-numbered series of twenty potsherds during the Mohammedan invasion of Egypt.

Although most of the *ostraka* are not of Christian origin, it is remarkable that many of them appear to be strongly influenced by the phraseology of the Greek Bible. It is significant that the potsherd letters very frequently request the loan of books from some more fortunate possessor of a library, and doubtless these books were often the Greek Septuagint or the New Testament.

Finally, the potsherds go some way towards filling one of the biggest gaps in our knowledge of the domestic life of antiquity. It is remarkable how little we are told in ancient literature about children, and what little we learn is invariably from the point of view of their elders. This is true even of the Bible, and it is only in the potsherds and other non-literary fragments that we get for the first time a vivid picture of Childhood as it really was in and about the time when Jesus Himself was a child.

Amongst the *ostraka* are many that were used as slates in school, still preserving the unformed handwriting and quaint misspelling of their little scribes. Some of the sherds, containing copy-book texts from well-known classical authors, were doubtless carried home for mother to admire, and so have found their way to a longevity beyond even mother's fondest dreams, in the museums of the modern world. In many cases, on the other hand, the caustic comments of the schoolmaster can still be seen, such as : *Enoch, don't throw your pen about !* Poor little Enoch, he little thought his schoolboy prank would be remembered for two thousand years !

VIII

NEW LIGHT FROM THE PAPYRI

*Is there anything whereof it may be said, See, this is new?
It hath been already of old time, which was before us.—*
(Ecclesiastes i, 10.)

OF all the discoveries which have thrown light upon the
background of the New Testament, it would be
difficult to name any of more interest, variety, or importance
than the numerous fragments of inscribed papyrus turned
up by the spade towards the end of the last century.* For
in ' the papyri,' as they are familiarly called, we have actual
documents, letters, and written scraps of all sorts, preserved
for us intact by the bone-dry sands of Egypt, just as they
left the writers' hands or were thrown into his equivalent
for a waste-paper basket two thousand years ago. The
paper is almost as white and smooth as ever it was, the ink
seems scarcely dry, the colour of the flowers sometimes
pressed between the sheets has scarcely faded, and it is even
said that a faint trace of their fragrance remains, so jealously
has the desert strong-room guarded its treasures from the
taint of Time.

THE PAPYRI DISCOVERIES

Papyrus, as everyone knows, served as the ' paper ' of
the ancient world. Its substance and manufacture, however,
were very different from modern paper. The *Cyperus*

---

* For this chapter consult A. Deissmann : *New Light from the Ancient East*, or (a
shorter summary) M. Van Rhyn : *Treasures of the Dust*.

Papyrus is a marsh plant growing in shallow water with roots as thick as a man's arm. It reaches to a height of ten to eighteen feet, waving a beautiful plume, and containing within its triangular-sectioned stalk a spongy pith. When dry, this pith was cut into very thin yet tough strips, which were laid over one another criss-cross, and fixed into position with adhesive. The joints were then smoothed over with pumice stone, so that a white polished level-surfaced sheet, eminently suited for writing upon with pen and ink, resulted.

The sheets thus prepared were at first gummed together in rolls extending to twenty, thirty or even forty yards in length, but later (in the case of Christian manuscripts, from the early second century)* were sewn together in codex form, that is to say like the pages of a modern book, the measurements of the page varying from about small ' octavo ' to ' quarto ' size. The common use of papyrus as writing material began in Egypt about 3000 B.C., spread to the whole of the civilized world by about 500 B.C., and continued down to the fourth century of the Christian era, when it became gradually displaced by vellum, parchment, and eventually paper† itself. As a writing material papyrus, therefore, has a very long history.

Thousands of ancient papyri manuscripts have been found stored in jars, chests, coffins, the bodies of mummified animals, and so on, while hundreds of thousands of fragments have been recovered from the wrappings of mummies, the bodies of mummified animals, the refuse-heaps of antiquity, and the like. The great majority of these finds were made in Egypt, particularly in Middle Egypt (the Fayyum), at places like Arsinoë, Memphis, Hawara, Hermopolis, and especially Oxyrhynchus, where both climate, sand and

* F. Kenyon : *Our Bible and the Ancient Manuscripts* (1939), p. 12.
† Paper was introduced into Greece by Arab traders from Damascus in the eleventh century.

religious custom combined to assure them exceptional chances of survival. But the languages in which they are written are representative of nearly the whole of the ancient world—Egyptian Demotic and Coptic, Hebrew and Aramaic, Arabic, Persian, Greek, Latin, and others.

The papyri attracted little attention in the early days of archæology, being looked upon as mere scraps of waste-paper, or as emanating chiefly from the decadent Hellenic and Roman periods of Egyptian history. Thus the importance of the discoveries made in 1840 at Memphis and in 1877 at Arsinoë was not realized till long afterwards, many thousands of precious documents being carelessly, even deliberately, destroyed. It is said that they were actually burnt by the peasants for the sake of their aromatic smell ! In 1890, however, Petrie's discovery of a possibly autograph manuscript of Aristotle's *Constitution of Athens*, a work hitherto believed to be non-extant, aroused a new interest in the possibilities of ' Papyrology.' And when Grenfell and Hunt in 1897 began sending home to England huge crates (some of them a ton in weight) packed with papyrus documents, the serious study of this virtually new material began in earnest.

We are not concerned here with the ancient Egyptian or the new Classical texts that emerged, nor yet with the myriads of third century and subsequent documents throwing light on the early Christian Church and the Mohammedan conquest. We must here confine ourselves chiefly to the evidence of the earlier papyri relevant to New Testament times. And we shall find abundant material for our purpose.

It is true that most of the papyri in question were found not in the Holy Land, but in Egypt, and that allowance for this should be made when applying their evidence to

Palestine and the Levant. But it was an Egypt impregnated with the Græco-Latin culture which pervaded the whole of the Near East, and the cultural link between Egypt and Palestine had always been particularly strong. Egypt was also at this period one of the great strongholds of the Jewish Dispersion, and in many ways it was a typical province among the provinces such as Syria, and Palestine, which composed the Roman Empire. It is probable that if Palestine itself had been as generous as Egypt in disgorging papyri, the discoveries would not have differed very materially from the Greek papyri found in the Fayyum. So that from this one section of the ancient Near East we can form a fairly accurate picture of the whole.

The evidence of the papyri falls broadly speaking under two heads illuminating the background of the New Testament first on its literary, and secondly on its human side.

THE NEW TESTAMENT AS LITERATURE

1. *ITS FORM.*—Amongst the papyri are several complete ' books,' both long and short, which give us a fair idea of what the original manuscripts of the New Testament must have looked like as they left the writers' hands. There can be little doubt that Matthew, Mark, Luke, John, Paul and the rest used just the same ink and just the same ' paper ' as this, and that when the work was finished it was ' bound ' in just the same way. When S. Paul asked S. Timothy to bring with him ' the books ' (II Timothy iv, 13), he must have been referring to precisely such roll-volumes, written in the same language and at the same date, as can be seen to-day in the British Museum and elsewhere. As an example of the general appearance of a first-century private

letter written on papyrus, now in the British Museum, see Plate VIII.*

All this has more than a sentimental or curiosity-value, for it must needs be taken into consideration by the textual critics. It would be an anachronism, for instance, to suggest that S. Luke's so-called ' Great Omission ' from S. Mark's Gospel was caused by his accidentally turning over two pages of that Gospel at once, for it seems that codices (page-books) were not in use in the first century. On the other hand, much might be explained by the limitations in the length of an ordinary papyrus roll (especially for writers in comparatively poor circumstances), or by the obvious tendency of the outermost layer of the roll (that is to say the *beginning* or Protocol of the book) to become frayed or torn away. It is probable that only in very few cases has what we might call the ' Title Page ' of a New Testament book been preserved, so that most of them (as is well known) have neither title nor author's name—the present ascriptions having been added in much later times. A similar mutilation through wear and tear might also have caused defects in the end or Colophon of the roll, where it was gummed occasionally to a rounded stick. In this case it would be the final paragraphs of the book which would be missing, as for instance perhaps in the Gospel of S. Mark as we have it to-day.

Of great importance, too, is the opportunity we now have of studying the actual script, spelling, punctuation and handwriting in vogue throughout the Greek-speaking world of New Testament times. Individual signatures differ, of course, but every age has its characteristic ' calligraphy ' or manner of writing, as anyone can see by comparing his Victorian grandmother's handwriting with

* A. Deissmann : *Light from the Ancient East*, p. 174.

that of his neo-Georgian daughter. S. Paul's handwriting, when he wrote ' See with how large letters I have written unto you with mine own hand ' (Galatians vi, 11, R.V.), cannot have been very different from that of the first-century papyri, especially, perhaps, those (there are many examples) which were written by Greek-speaking *Jews*. The textual critic of to-day knows (within obvious limits) how the New Testament writers formed their letters, numerals, capitals, abbreviations and the rest, and, in consequence, just the kind of mistakes in copying which might subsequently have been made.

Upon the Epistles of the New Testament, in particular, a very strong light is thrown by the innumerable examples of contemporary Greek letters and personal correspondence found among the papyri. So great is the relevant material that we can now definitely ' place ' the Epistles in this or that clearly marked category. First there are the highly polished and deliberately literary productions, like the Epistle to the Hebrews, which is rather a doctrinal treatise than an Epistle. Secondly, we have less formal documents addressed to particular persons or groups of persons, clearly not intended as permanent contributions to ' literature,' yet written with more dignity and careful consideration than is usual in a purely private letter. Amongst such we might include the Epistles to the Corinthians, or Galatians. Finally, there is the more intimate and personal correspondence, like the Epistle to Philemon.

Examples of all these types have been found. We realize now that S. Paul did not *invent* the Epistle method of dealing with his converts. Other religions beside Christianity had their letter-writing missionaries. We have, for instance, an Epistle of Zoilus, an ' apostle ' (if we may call him so) of the god Serapis, addressed to Apollonius of

Alexandria. It is written, like all the papyri quoted in this chapter, in the Greek language, and begins in much the same way as S. Paul's letters : *Zoilus the Aspendian to Apollonius, Greeting*. Zoilus, like S. Paul, writes on behalf of his ' church,' considers himself divinely commissioned, prays to be delivered from sickness, but is ready to suffer if such be the Divine will ; apologizes for not coming as quickly to visit his flock as he had intended, prays for his fellow-workers, and so on. Yet under these superficial resemblances, how great is the contrast ! Zoilus' letter, in effect, is no more than a speciously-worded request for money : *Be not stricken with terror at the expense, as being of great cost to thee*, he ends, *nay, it shall be to thee of great profit, for I will look to everything. Farewell.*

It is in the atmosphere, rather than in the details, of such correspondence that one is made to realize both how typical and yet how gloriously unique are the letters of the New Testament. Unfortunately, a point of this kind can only be made by somewhat extensive quotations, for which we have no space, and so must leave it.

One short letter, however, may be quoted in part as an example from Egypt of S. Paul's habit of employing a scribe or amanuensis to write the bulk of his letters for him :— *Asclepiades, to Portis, Greeting. I have received from you the rent for the field I leased to you for the year* 25, *and you now owe me nothing. Written at dictation of the above by Eumelus, who was asked to do so because Asclepiades writes rather slowly.* The amanuensis or scribe who wrote the letter was evidently not above inserting a little of his own, as we see also in S. Paul's Epistles : for example, *I, Tertius, who write the epistle, salute you* (Romans xvi, 22). Actually to write a letter with one's own hand was an exceptional mark of favour, a fact which lends point to S. Paul's note at the end of his Epistle to the Galatians : *See with how large letters I have written unto you with mine own hand* (Galatians vi, 11, R.V.).   Compare also a similar personal ending to the Epistle to the Corinthians, Colossians, etc., and his statement : *The salutation of me Paul with mine own hand, which is the token in every epistle* (II Thessalonians iii, 17, R.V.).

2. *ITS LANGUAGE.*—Perhaps the most important concrete and direct addition made by the papyri to our understanding of the New Testament has been in the linguistic sphere. As the material accumulates we realize almost with dismay how very little was really known at the end of the nineteenth century about the syntax and vocabulary of first-century Greek.   Approaching the New Testament with a Liddell-and-Scott Lexicon of Classical Greek, we were like foreigners trying to understand a modern newspaper with the aid of Dr. Johnson's Dictionary !

It is not only that we now understand the significance of many words and phrases which were once obscure, but we no longer affect the old attitude of academic disdain towards the sacred text.   Thirty years ago the Classical master who took us through our Greek Testament used to warn us against its ' bad Greek.'   We were bidden to remember that the Apostles were ' ignorant and unlearned men ' (Acts iv, 13), and were moreover writing in a tongue foreign to them, so that of course one could not expect the Greek of the Gospels to be up to Sixth Form standard !   Declensions and conjugations were haphazard, idioms were Jewish, and new words had been arbitrarily invented for the new ideas of Christianity.

All this was wrong, or at least exaggerated, and it affected not only our understanding of the text but our opinion of the writers.

To-day we realize that the Evangelists and S. Paul were writing, like sensible men, primarily to be understood by their readers. The papyri, written in precisely the same language for precisely the same kind of people, have shown us that New Testament Greek is neither a specially devised ecclesiastical language, nor a local dialect ; still less is it an archaistic revival of Classical Attic Greek ; it is simply the ordinary spoken Greek of the first-century man-in-the-street. ' The great fact that impresses the investigator of the non-literary inscriptions and papyri is that the New Testament speaks practically the same language as was spoken by simple and unlearned men in the Imperial age.'[*]

It was, in short, what the Prayer Book would call the ' vulgar tongue,' or what Deissmann has taught us to call the *Koiné* (κοίνη, common speech), a kind of universal language or *Lingua Franca*, spoken and ' understanded of the people,' whatever local language (such as Phrygian, Latin, or Aramaic) they might speak as well, throughout the Roman Empire.

Deissmann is never tired of pointing the significance of this. ' How completely the splendid simplicity and homeliness of the New Testament fulfils Our Lord's ideal that " the poor have the Gospel preached unto them " (S. Luke vii, 22). We may apply to the popular language of the *Koiné*, in relation to the *literary* language of the day, those words of the Master : " Consider the lilies of the field, how they grow—yet even Solomon in all his glory was not like unto one of these " (S. Matthew vi, 28).'

The papyri have also explained the precise significance of many words in Koiné Greek, which were once either entirely absent from the Classical dictionaries, or else were incorrectly supposed to have the same meaning in the first century as

* A. Deissmann : *New Light on the New Testament*, p. 27.

they had in the Golden Age of Demosthenes, the famous Athenian orator.

In the old days it was estimated that at least 10 per cent. (500 or more) of the words used in the New Testament were specially invented by, or at least peculiar to the Biblical writers. Often the Commentary used to say of this or that word that it was a ἅπαξ λεγόμενον (that is to say, unique, not found anywhere else), so that one could only guess at its meaning. To-day we know from their appearance in the papyri, that nearly all these words were in common use among the people of the day. Definitions of them are given in the papyri, or the context makes their meaning clear, so that it has been possible at last to compile a complete dictionary of New Testament Greek,* wherein actual examples of the use of such words is given from contemporary documents.

The subject is too technical to elaborate here, but we may give a few examples. Ἀλλογενής (foreigner) was not found outside the Bible until it appeared on the Temple inscription already noted (p. 73). The following are also words which were once marked as ' Peculiar to the Bible,' or ' Only in the New Testament,' but which have been found in ordinary first-century Greek as exemplified in the papyri. ὀνικός (of a millstone), κόκκινος (scarlet), ἱματίζω (clothe), ὀπτάνομαι (am seen), ἐλλογῶ (impute), ἀναστατῶ (stir up), ἀφιλάργυρος (not covetous), αὐθεντεῖν (to have dominion over), διαταγή (ordinance), πρωτότοκος (first-born), κατήγωρ (accuser), ἀναθεματίζω (curse), ἀρχιποίμην (chief shepherd), προσκαρτέρησις (perseverance), ἐπισυναγώγη (assembly).

To these we may add λογία (a church -collection), hitherto found only in I Corinthians xvi, 1, 2, but now known

* e.g. J. H. Moulton and A. Milligan : *Dictionary of New Testament Greek* (1914) and A. T. Robertson : *Grammar of the Greek New Testament in the Light of Historical Research* (1914).

to have been a common term for collections (' offertories ') made in the pagan Temples. When Our Lord commanded His Apostles to *Take nothing for your journey, save a staff only ; no bread, no wallet, no money* (S. Mark vi, 8, R.V.), the word for ' wallet ' (πήρα) which was once thought to mean a portmanteau, is now known to mean a mendicant's collecting bag. In the phrase *They have their reward* the word for have (ἀπέχω) really means ' they have got a receipt for payment in full.' The word for ' daily ' (ἐπιούσιος) in the Lord's Prayer, long a puzzle to the commentators, has been found in an ancient housekeeping book referring to the daily order for bread.

Many of the common phrases and idioms of the New Testament have been paralleled from the papyri. To give but two or three examples : S. Paul says of Aquila and Priscilla that *For my life they laid down their own necks* (τὸν ἑαύτων τράχηλον ὑπέθηκαν) (Romans xvi, 4), now known to be a popular expression for self-sacrificing devotion. Our Lord tells His followers to *Beware of*, literally to ' look out for ' (βλέπειν ἄπο) the Scribes and Pharisees, in the same terms as an Alexandrian business man of A.D. 41 writes to his partner to ' look out for those Jews.' Converts to the Faith are baptized *Into His Name* (εἰς τὸ ὄνομα αὐτοῦ), a current phrase for transferance of ownership. The disciples are sent forth *By two and two* (S. Mark vi, 7), a curiously ungrammatical expression (δύο δύο, literally ' two, two '), yet frequently in use. The nominative case of ' full ' in S. John's phrase *Full of grace and truth* (S. John i, 14) long defied parsing, until the papyri showed that by the first century the word ' full ' (πλήρης) had become virtually indeclinable.

One last, but particularly interesting, example of grammatical difficulties thus cleared up is in S. Matthew xxvi, 50, where Our Lord says to Judas words which, literally translated, are ' Friend, for that-which art-thou-here ? ' (ἑταῖρε, ἐφ' ὃ πάρει). ' That-which ' (ὅ) is a relative pronoun, not an interrogative, so the R.V. rendered it *Friend, do that for which thou art come.* But Deissmann has shown that the phrase was common in colloquial Greek, being almost the exact equivalent of our ' What are you here for ? ' So that the Authorised Version, with its *Friend, wherefore art thou come?* was right after all (see p. 29).

It was a little unfortunate, in fact, that the scholars did not wait another thirty years or so before undertaking their revised translation of the New Testament. Had they done so, the discoveries of papyrology would have saved them from several needless alterations and inaccurate renderings of the Greek.

THE GENERAL BACKGROUND

1. *SOCIAL CONDITIONS.*—More interesting to the general reader is the very full and varied picture which the papyri give us of life and civilization in the first-century Roman Empire. Amazingly modern it all is ! Here is a fragment of an ancient butcher's bill ; there a Coroner's finding in a case of suspected suicide ; an invitation to a wedding breakfast ; a membership ticket of an athletic club ; and an inventory of household goods, all jotted down at the very time when our Lord or His Apostles were living amongst just the sort of people who wrote these papyri scraps that lie before us.

Thus in A.D. 30, within a year of the Crucifixion, Demetrius in Egypt was writing a papyrus which still survives to immortalize his complaint about his wife's desertion. Another scrap, in which a grocer gives his undertaking not to sell eggs below the market price, was written in A.D. 32, conceivably on the very day that S. Stephen was stoned to death. In A.D. 49, while S. Paul and S. Barnabas were making notes, perhaps, on just the same kind of ' paper ' for their speech at the Council at Jerusalem, this memorandum which lies before us was made telling us that *A certain Pesuris in the seventh year of our Sovereign Claudius Cæsar, picked up a foundling in the gutter*.

There are Trade Union regulations, Burial Club receipts, Tax-collectors' demand notes, Death certificates, Letters of condolence, Letters of abuse, in fact almost every kind of writing under the sun. ' The contents of these non-literary fragments,' writes Deissmann, ' are as varied as life itself. The papyrus is something much more lifelike than inscriptions in stone—which are often as cold and lifeless as the stone that bears them. We see the men who wrote them ; we gaze into the nooks and crannies of private life, for which history has no eyes and the historian no spectacles. These plain unpretentious scraps of papyrus come as a stream of new, warm blood reanimating the history of the times.'[*]

It is just this very *human* quality of the non-literary papyri which gives them their great value as the indispensable, almost the only, evidence which has come down to us of the everyday life of ordinary unimportant people, such as were the majority of those who composed the Christian congregations of New Testament days. It is hopeless to look for notice of first-century Christianity in the formal literature of the day, unless we include the New Testament itself in that category. Only in these ephemeral letters and memoranda retrieved from the waste-paper baskets of humble homes can one meet face to face the ' weary and heavy laden ' to whom the Cross appealed.

* A. Deissmann : *New Light on the New Testament*, p. 17.

In our last chapter we referred to the new light shed by the *ostraka* on Children in the ancient world. There is much more to the same effect in the papyri. The letter of Theonas to his father is justly famous, and worth repeating almost in full. The boy is disappointed that his father has gone to Alexandria without him, and writes to tell him so in no uncertain terms. The spelling, like the handwriting, is that of the eternal schoolboy!

Theonas to his father Theon, Greeting. This is a nice thing you've done, not taking me with you to Town. If you refoose to take me with you to Alexandria, I'll not write to you, nor speke to you, nor hope you are well. . . . When you refoose to take me with you, this is what happens—even mother told Archelaus that I was a nuisance, hang him! And thanks a lot for that present you sent me—big locust-beans! They quite took me in that day, when you set sale! But do please send for me. If you don't send, I'll go on hunger strike, that's all! Farewell.

Another boy writes lamenting the death of his favourite fighting cock : *For its sake have I been called great in my life, and considered lucky. . . . I am at a loss where to go. I have a good mind to put an end to myself!*

There are many examples of schoolboys' copybooks, or perhaps impositions. In one papyrus the first line of Demosthenes' great speech, the *De Corona*, is copied out over and over again. One boy adds a note to his exercise : *Good luck to him who reads this!* Another boy writes to his father (evidently in connection with his school report !) : *Don't worry about my mathematics ; I'm working hard.* One exceptionally long-headed schoolboy begs that his teacher may be well fed, so that he may be better tempered !

There is a pretty letter from a little girl to her absent father : *Ammonous to her sweetest father, Greeting. Now*

L

that I have got your letter and have learnt that by the will of the gods you have been kept safe, I am very glad, and finding opportunity the same hour I have written you this letter hastening to greet you. All the family send you greetings. Farewell.

There are also many letters from parents to their children. One mother writes to her son, who had injured his foot, *Do not forget, my child, to write to me about your health. You know how anxious mother is about her boy.* And there is the very elder-brother-like letter addressed by Sempronius to his brother Maximus : *I hear you are not very obliging to mother. Please, dearest brother, do not vex her. If any of the youngsters disobey her, give them a box on the ears. You are the eldest at home now, so you are in charge. Don't be offended if I write to you like this.*

But the general interest of the papyri, illuminating as they do every class of people and every department of human life, must not tempt us to linger unduly in this seductive by-path. We must hurry on to those which more directly concern the New Testament.

2. *NEW TESTAMENT PARALLELS.*—Many examples have survived of ' Books of Magic ' such as were burnt at Ephesus in response to the denunciations of S. Paul (Acts xix, 19). Of these, the most celebrated is the ' Great Magical Papyrus ' now in Paris, which, although considerably later than our period (it was written about A.D. 300), is evidently a compilation from previous works on the subject. It is, of course, a farrago of the purest nonsense, like the specimen already quoted (p. 123), and very long. One brief extract will suffice : *For those possessed by evil spirits, an approved charm by Pibechis is as follows : Take oil made from unripe olives, with herb mastic and lotus pith, and boil it with marjoram, saying Joel, Ossarthiomi, Emori, Theochipsoith, Sithemeoch,*

Sothe, Joe, Mimipsothiooph, Phersothi, A,E,I,O,U, come out of kim ! (The words are gibberish.)

Further light on the Census of S. Luke II (see index) is added by a papyrus copy of the Edict of G. Vibius Maximus, Governor of Egypt in A.D. 104.   It will be remembered that the Gospel states that every citizen had to return to his native town for enrolment—a statement which was questioned by the older commentators. This papyrus Edict, however, runs : *The enrolment by householders being at hand, it is necessary to notify all who for any cause soever are outside their nomes* [districts] *to return to their domestic hearths, that they may accomplish the customary method of enrolment.* Ramsay adduces this as supporting S. Luke. The chief purpose of the Roman Census was, of course, to assess the poll tax and other personal dues payable to the Government.   Among the papyri there is a large number of documents relating to these assessments (see p. 152).

Interesting in themselves, and highly illustrative of the subject matter of the New Testament are parallels to it which appear in the papyri. Imprisonment for debt, for instance, is frequently mentioned. Pilate's release of Barabbas (S. Mark xv, 15) is recalled by a fragment in which a governor of Egypt, G. Septimius Vegetus, says to his prisoner : *Thou hast been worthy of scourging, but I will give thee to the people.* The price of sparrows (S. Matthew x, 29) is given in a papyrus price list.   The supposed cure of a blind man (cf. S. John ix, 7) is described : *To Valerius Aper, a blind soldier, the god Æsculapius revealed that he should go and take blood of a white cock, together with honey, and anoint his eyes three days.   And he received his sight, and came and gave thanks publicly to the god.*

The story of the man who fell among thieves on the road to Jericho (S. Luke x, 30) is paralleled by the experiences of two merchants : *As we were returning about daybreak from the village of Theadelphia, certain malefactors came upon us between Polydeucia and Theadelphia, and tied us up, and assaulted us with many blows, and wounded Pasion, and robbed us of our property.* A letter from Antonius Longus to his widowed mother recalls another Prodigal Son who regretted leaving home : *I am ashamed to come home, for I go about in rags. I write to thee, because I am naked. I beseech thee, mother, forgive me. I know full well what I have brought upon myself. I have been punished, as I deserved. I know that I have sinned. I beseech thee* . . . (Here it breaks off). Just such a letter might the Prodigal Son (S. Luke xv, 11f) have written home on just such a piece of frayed papyrus retrieved from the gutter, in just the same ink, handwriting and colloquial Greek. If such a letter had been preserved, this is what it would look like.

When gathered together, in short, the papyri form the equivalent of a popular newspaper, giving us an insight into every department of first-century life as it appeared in the eyes of those who were actually living it.

3. *THE RELIGIOUS BACKGROUND.*—Lastly, though here is a subject that must be drastically compressed, the papyri throw a strangely revealing light upon the religious and mental background of the New Testament—what people really believed and thought behind the scenes.

Perhaps the most surprising discovery in this sphere is that many of the characteristic expressions of the early Church were by no means peculiar to Christianity. Far from being freshly-coined 'cult-phrases' peculiar to the new Faith, they were often just bold adoptions or adaptations of expressions already familiar in the pagan world.

Most of the terms expressing the Divinity of Christ, for example, had already been applied in popular usage to the

Roman Emperor. The papyri make it plain that in the Near East at all events the worship of the Emperor as a Divine Being was established far earlier than we had supposed. S. Paul had foreseen that the Man of Sin, *He who opposeth and exalteth himself above all that is called god, or that is worshipped* shall be found *setting himself forth as God*. (II Thessalonians ii, 4) and even as the words were written it was happening.

As early as 48 B.C. an inscription of Ephesus salutes Julius Cæsar as *God made manifest . . . the Saviour of human life*. A papyrus acknowledges Augustus in his first year as *God of God*, and his birthday is spoken of as *The Nativity of the God*. During his lifetime, he bears the title *Son of God*. As early as 9 B.C. he is called *Divine*. Nero (of all men !) is even more highly honoured ; he is called *The Good God !*

When the Christians confessed Jesus Christ as ' LORD ' they were deliberately claiming full Divinity for their Master, and for Him alone. But the Romans had already made the same claim for their Emperor. Augustus officially refused this Oriental exaggeration of flattery, but a papyrus of A.D. 1 calls him *God and Lord*. Other inscriptions show that the title was given also to Tiberius and (in the feminine, *Lady*) his mother Livia, to Caius Caligula, and to Claudius, despite their disclaimers. With Nero ' the number of examples rushes up tremendously ; everywhere, down to the remotest village, the officials call Nero " LORD " ' (Deissmann) —a fact, incidentally, noted by S. Luke (Acts xxv, 26). By the time of Domitian, ' LORD ' had become a recognized title of the Emperor-god, and Christians were being martyred for refusing to concede it to him.

Similarly, the term *Saviour* and *Saviour of the World* was applied to the Emperors. Even the word *Gospel*, that is to say Good Tidings, was no new thing ; *The Nativity of the Divine Augustus was for the world the beginning of the Gospel on his account*, we read in one fulsome papyrus. So too the words *Advent* and *Epiphany* were used in connection with the Emperor's state visit to a city, ' Advent ' coins being struck, and ' Epiphany ' sacrifices being offered in his honour. The title *Holy Scriptures* was given to the decrees of the Emperor long before it was applied to the New Testament. And so on. For the first time we realize the real reason for the growing antagonism of the first-century Church towards Rome. There could be no compromise with a State which made itself equal with God.

The religious witness of the papyri in general testifies to a universal earnest, but ignorant and bewildered, groping after some religion, any religion, which should afford a way of escape from the emptiness of mere living to the Fullness of Life. S. Paul hit on the truth when he observed that the Greeks were ' religious ' *au fond*, but ' worshipped in ignorance an unknown god ' (Acts xvii, 22f, R.V.Marg.) ' If we wish to be just,' writes Deissmann, ' our verdict as historians of religion must be framed like this : that the vast majority of mankind were not tired of religion, nor hostile to religion, but friendly to it, and hungering for it.'* When they could be persuaded to listen to the Gospel of Christ they quickly realised that the Desire of the Nations had come.

* A. Deissmann : *New Light on the New Testament*, p. 74.

IX

EARLY CHRISTIAN DOCUMENTS

And there are also many other things which Jesus did, the
which, if they should be written every one, I suppose that
even the world itself could not contain the books that
should be written.—(S. John xxi, 25.)

IT is a little disappointing, perhaps, that among all the
numerous first-century papyri so far discovered, few, if
any, can be said to bear the stamp of distinctively Christian
origin, despite the fact that there must have been many
converts at this time in North Africa and Egypt. Nothing
is impossible in archæology, however, and we may yet
stumble upon a fragment written by someone who had
actually seen the Lord, or who had spoken (maybe) with
him who is traditionally credited with missionary work in
Egypt, the Evangelist S. Mark.

In the meantime, we can at any rate claim this for the
papyri, that among them are numbered by far the earliest
Christian manuscripts in existence, documents which go
back in some cases as far as the middle of the second
century, and which might therefore have been written by
men who had actually seen S. John the Apostle in his old
age. If there are few that can be dated quite as early as
this, yet there are many which emanate from the later
second, third, and early fourth centuries, and are thus
considerably older than the oldest vellum manuscripts of
the New Testament yet discovered.

OLDEST MANUSCRIPTS OF THE NEW TESTAMENT

Up to the end of the nineteenth century the Codex Sinaiticus (א, Aleph) was believed to be the oldest manuscript of the complete New Testament in existence, with the Codex Vaticanus (B) (incomplete) perhaps a few years older still.* The publication of these famous codices in the middle of the nineteenth century made an epoch in textual research, resulting eventually in Westcott and Hort's Greek Testament, and the Revised Version of 1885. They were written on vellum (skin) in archaic uncials (capital letters), and were centuries older than the manuscripts upon which the Authorized Version of A.D. 1611 had been based. Written about A.D. 330, these ancient uncials carried the text of the New Testament as far back as the establishment of the Christian Church under Constantine, a date which coincided with the introduction of vellum as a popular writing material. It seemed hopeless to look for anything earlier than this, so Codex א and Codex B were accepted as the final Court of Appeal.

But between these ancient manuscripts, copied in A.D. 330, and the actual New Testament archetypes (the original autographs as they left the writers' pens), composed before A.D. 100, there stretched a gap of nearly two hundred and fifty years. The links in the chain between Codex א and the nineteenth century were complete, being represented by literally thousands of manuscripts, but the only way one could ' check up ' on the continuity of the Greek text during those missing two hundred and fifty years was by re-translating the Old Latin, Syriac, and other versions back into Greek, or by comparing the Scriptural quotations

* For the Manuscripts of the New Testament read F. Kenyon : *Our Bible and the Ancient Manuscripts* (1939). For the Codex Sinaiticus see British Museum booklet : *The Mount Sinai Manuscript of the Bible* (1934).

found in the early Fathers and other writers of the Church. This gap has not been completely bridged by the papyri, but they have narrowed it down by at least a hundred years.

In 1897 a papyrus was discovered which brought as much joy to the heart of New Testament scholars as any archæological discovery yet made.* It was a page from S. Matthew's Gospel torn out of a papyrus codex, and written in uncials at a date about A.D. 230, being thus a whole century older than the oldest manuscripts of the New Testament then known. It carried us far back behind Constantine's establishment of the Church, behind the earliest ' authorized editions ' of the sacred text, and turning away from great *editions de luxe* officially made for use in church, it showed us a page or two of an ordinary private pocket Testament.

This precious papyrus contains only a portion of the first chapter of the Gospel (S. Matthew i, 1–20), but how· eagerly the scholars scanned that faded scrap of paper to see if it supported the text of the Codex Sinaiticus ! And it did ! The trusted Codex stood the test well, so that, assuming the whole to be on a level with the part, it could be credited with the preservation of readings that were at least a hundred years older than the time when it was written. We say ' at least,' for it is obvious that the papyrus fragment itself must have been based on a still earlier manuscript of the text, and one which had been accepted by the Church as an accurate version of the original Gospel. In other words, the Greek text of our Revised Version could be traced back in essentials to the middle of the second century or thereabouts, and a kind of ' apostolic succession ' had been established for it.

This fragment of S. Matthew was only the beginning of

* C. M. Cobern : *New Archæological Discoveries,* p. 132ff.

good things. Quite recently (in 1930) the announcement of the discovery of what are called the ' Chester Beatty Papyri '* caused quite a stir amongst Biblical scholars. This famous collection contains portions of several papyri codices of the New Testament ranging in date from the third to the fourth or fifth century of our era. Three of the codices contain portions of the Gospels, the Acts, the Pauline Epistles, and the Revelation. One of them consists of thirty leaves of a codex which originally contained all four Gospels and the Acts. ' They appear to be of the third century,' observes Dr. Guppy† (Librarian of the Rylands Library which specializes in such things), ' and consequently are about a century earlier than the Codex Sinaiticus.'

Since the discovery of this important collection a yet older New Testament papyrus has been found (in 1935) dating as far back as the early second century. It is a small fragment of a codex containing a portion of the Gospel of S. John (c. xviii, 31-33, 37, 38). Of this, now in the Rylands Library, Dr. Guppy writes :† ' It was written when the ink of the original autograph (A.D. 100) can scarcely have been dry. It must be regarded as the earliest fragment by at least fifty years of any portion of the New Testament ' (plate VIII). And again it gives general support to the text of the great uncial manuscripts.

There are many other Biblical papyri fragments, large and small, dating from the third and early fourth century, and thus helping to bridge the gap between the archetypes and the Codex Sinaiticus. Although certain differences of reading appear amongst them, as is inevitable with docu-

---

* F. Kenyon : *The Chester Beatty Biblical Papyri* (1937). The very oldest Biblical manuscript yet discovered is a fragment of the Septuagint version of Deuteronomy dated 150 B.C.

† *Transmission of the Bible* (Rylands Library (1935)).

ments copied out by hand, yet the general effect of the papyrus evidence is exceedingly reassuring. It is clear that the Revised text of our New Testament, based on the great uncial manuscripts of the fourth and fifth centuries, does in fact preserve a true version of the original. There is no reason to suppose that, if we were to find an actual archetype of any book of the New Testament still surviving intact in some dry cavity of stone or sand, it would differ materially from the version of it now appearing in our revised Greek Bibles.

LOST GOSPELS

Most people are so accustomed to the idea of four Gospels, Matthew, Mark, Luke and John, that the possibility of there having been any other accounts of our Lord's life never occurs to them. Yet, on reflection, it is hard to believe that of all the thousands of hearers who came under His influence, only these four should have committed anything to paper. S. Luke, indeed, informs us explicitly that it was not so. He tells us in his preface that many attempts to write a gospel had been made, before he started his own : *Forasmuch as many have taken in hand to draw up a narrative concerning those matters which have been fulfilled among us . . . it seemed good to me also, having traced the course of all things accurately from the first, to write unto thee in order, most excellent Theophilus.* (S. Luke i, 1, R.V.) In his Acts he even quotes a saying of our Lord which is not to be found in his own or any other of the ordinary Gospels : *Remember the words of the Lord Jesus, how He said, It is more blessed to give than to receive.* (Acts xx, 35.)

Amongst these forerunners, S. Luke probably included

the short gospel of S. Mark, which he seems to have had before him as he wrote, as well as the collection of Sayings of Christ now known to scholars as Q (Quelle). But he must almost certainly have had others in mind besides these, although up to the discovery of the papyri it was believed that any unknown ' gospel ' which might have existed in the first century had been for ever lost. There seemed little chance of adding anything from authentic contemporary sources to the information about our Lord and his Teaching which was already to be found in the ordinary ' canonical ' New Testament.

As to whether any such genuinely early ' Lost Gospels,' or fragments of them, can be identified among the papyri, opinions continue to differ, but extraordinarily interesting discoveries have been made.

Probably the very earliest fragment of a non-canonical ' Gospel ' is that discovered in Egypt as recently as 1934, now in the British Museum. It is written on two tattered leaves of a papyrus codex, and dated by its editor, Dr. H. Idris Bell, Keeper of the British Museum Manuscripts, as ' about the middle of the second century, more probably before than after A.D. 150.'* It was written, therefore, by one who (as far as dates go) might well have spoken with S. John the Divine during his last days in Ephesus (c. A.D. 100).

From the surviving extracts of this narrative, Dr. Bell inclines to believe that the author was not merely imitating the New Testament Gospels, but was ' following a stream of tradition independent both of S. John's Gospel and of the Synoptics (Matthew, Mark, and Luke).' It is probable, one has to remember, that this papyrus is itself a copy of an earlier manuscript, so that the original may even take

* H. I. Bell : *The New Gospel* (*Sunday Express*, March 24, 1935, and onwards).

us as far back as the 'narratives' mentioned by S. Luke in his preface.

It must be confessed that there is nothing very spectacular in the fresh information about our Lord which we gain from this fragment. One section gives an account of His dispute with the Rulers of the People in phrases which appear to be selected mainly from S. John's Gospel, *Turning to the rulers of the people, He spake this saying: Search the Scriptures in which ye think that ye have life: these are they which bear witness of Me. Think not that I came to accuse you to My Father:* etc. (cf. S. John v, 39). A second section tells of the Miracle of the Healing of the Leper, already well known from the canonical Gospels. A third contains the questioning of Jesus by the Herodians.

Only one small portion of the papyrus adds anything fresh to the Gospel story, and unfortunately this fragment is the most dilapidated and illegible of them all. No complete translation is, therefore, possible. Dr. Bell gives the following rendering ' of so much of the Greek as yields any sort of sense,' the words within brackets being inserted by conjecture: *When ye have shut up [a grain of corn] in [a hidden place], where it is secretly placed under [the earth], why does it increase so enormously in weight? And when they were perplexed at His strange question, Jesus, as He walked stood on the edge of the River Jordan, and stretching forth His right hand, He [took corn] and sprinkled it upon the [river]. And then [taking] water [on which the corn] had been sprinkled, [He cast it upon the land] before them, and it sent forth fruit. . . .*

Dr. Bell does not, of course, vouch for the conjectures in brackets; they may quite possibly misrepresent the situation altogether. In any case the fresh miracle (if it be a miracle) thus added to the Gospel Story of our Lord's life must remain of problematical authenticity.

Nevertheless, the papyrus has an important bearing upon textual criticism. While resembling in general the style and phraseology of S. John's Gospel, yet at the same time showing acquaintance with the other three Gospels, it attempts no slavish imitation of any of them, either in word or in subject matter. It is possible, indeed, that this ' Lost Gospel ' represents a text earlier than the canonical Gospels, or an independent compilation from the basic documents which were used so much more skilfully by the New Testament evangelists.

APOCRYPHAL GOSPELS

This brings us into touch with the so-called ' Apocryphal Gospels,' or rather (for it is an enormous subject, and mainly outside our scope), with the earliest examples of them. Most of the Apocryphal Gospels* were composed long after the New Testament had taken final shape, and though frequently named after Apostles—Peter, James, Thomas, etc.—their information is derived for the most part from an imaginative elaboration of the authentic Gospels, and they were never acknowledged as Scripture by the Church.

It is possible, however, that some of the earliest Apocryphal writers may have preserved here and there a genuine tradition which had failed for some reason or other to win a place in the official accounts of our Lord's life, so that any papyrus fragment of such literature dating from really early times has a certain interest for New Testament students.

A great sensation amongst scholars was caused in 1885

* See M. R. James : *The Apocryphal New Testament* (1924).

by the discovery in Middle Egypt of a long vellum fragment of the Gospel and Apocalypse of S. Peter. The manuscript itself dates only from the fourth century, but it is believed to represent an original going back to about A.D. 160. Its account of the Trial and Crucifixion of Christ shows knowledge of all the four canonical Gospels, but adds certain details of its own. Most of them, however, seem to be no more than such natural insertions as might occur to anyone meditating on the Passion Story. For instance, *They took the Lord, and pushed Him as they ran ;* and again during the Three Hours' Darkness *Many went about with lamps, supposing it to be night time.*

Another interesting discovery was that by Grenfell and Hunt in 1903 of an apocryphal Gospel fragment dating from the third century, though representing an original going back, it is thought, as far as A.D. 140. On examination, however, it is seen to contain nothing more startling than a paraphrase of the Sermon on the Mount, in the style of the following : *Take no thought from morning until evening, nor from evening until morning, either for your food, what ye shall eat, or for your raiment, what ye shall put on,* and so forth.

Mention may also be made of a papyrus codex of the well-known apocryphal ' Acts of Paul ' discovered by Reinhardt in 1896. The original book was composed perhaps as early as A.D. 160 and though denounced by Tertullian as a forgery was highly honoured by the early church, as preserving a genuine tradition about S. Paul's conversion of S. Thecla in Iconium.

NEW SAYINGS OF CHRIST

More interesting still are the papyri which report various Lost Sayings, or ' Logia ' of our Lord—sayings, that is, which are not recorded in the New Testament. No one can read the scriptural account of our Lord's utterances without realizing that He must have said a great deal more than is reported in the Gospels, and every Christian naturally pricks up his ears at the suggestion that further Sayings of our Lord have been discovered.

It has long been agreed by scholars that a written anthology or memorandum (usually called Q) of our Lord's Sayings, translated from Aramaic into Greek, was in existence at a very early date, and was used in the compilation both of S. Matthew's and of S. Luke's Gospels. What one would like above all to find is, of course, a papyrus containing this document in the original Aramaic, but there is nothing unlikely in the supposition that other collections of Sayings besides Q might have been in existence written in Greek, and that such collections might still survive amongst the papyri of Egypt.

There are some who think that such a Collection, or rather a third-century copy of it, can be recognized in the remarkable papyrus (a codex leaf) containing ' Sayings of Jesus ' dug up by Grenfell and Hunt at Oxyrhynchus in 1896.* We will call it Papyrus A, to distinguish it from a second papyrus which was discovered subsequently. Its contents are as follows :—

PAPYRUS A.

1. . . . *And then shalt thou see clearly to cast out the mote that is in thy brother's eye.*

2. *Jesus saith, Except ye fast to the world, ye shall in no wise find the Kingdom of God ; and except ye make the Sabbath a real Sabbath, ye shall not see the Father.*

3. *Jesus saith, I stood in the midst of the world, and in*

* Grenfell and Hunt: *Sayings of Our Lord* (1897).

*the flesh was I seen of them ; and I found all men drunken,
and none found I athirst among them, and My soul grieveth
over the sons of men, because they are blind in their hearts,
and see not. . . .*

4. *. . . Poverty . . .*

5. *Jesus saith, Wherever there are two, they are not
without God ; and wherever there is one alone, I say, I am
with him. Raise the stone, and there thou shalt find Me ;
cleave the wood, and there am I.*

6. *Jesus saith, A prophet is not acceptable in his own
country, neither does a physician work cures upon them that
know him.*

7. *Jesus saith, A city built upon the top of a high hill and
established can neither fall nor be hid.*

8. *Jesus saith, Thou hearest with one ear, but . . .*

These Sayings in their original form are believed to
date as early as the beginning of the second century, and
might therefore have been written down by men who had
received them from actual disciples of Jesus. Some of
them are striking utterances, appealing to one's instinct
as the sort of thing our Lord might well have said.
Linguistically, the Greek does not, as is the case with so
many of the later supposed ' Sayings of Jesus,' preclude the
possibility of an Aramaic original, although it can be
paralleled often enough by phrases in the early Fathers and
the Apocryphal Gospels. It has been pointed out, in
favour of a very early date, that these Sayings contain no
reference to any of the acute controversies which began to
disturb the Church towards the end of the first century.
On the whole, they deserve serious consideraton as a
possibly authentic recollection transmitted from the earliest
Church.

A second papyrus collection of Sayings was found (also

M

by Grenfell and Hunt) at Oxyrhynchus in 1903.* It consists of forty-two lines of Greek on the back of a roll-form Property Survey of about A.D. 300, but is believed to be a copy of an original dating back to the early second century. This papyrus runs as follows :—

PAPYRUS B.

Heading :

These are the wonderful words which Jesus the living Lord spake unto . . . and Thomas. And He saith unto them, Everyone that hearkens to these words shall never taste of death.

The Sayings :

1. *Jesus saith, Let not him who seeks . . . cease until he finds, and when he finds, he shall be astonished ; astonished he shall reach the Kingdom ; and having reached the Kingdom he shall rest.*

2. *Jesus saith, Ye ask, who are those that draw us to the Kingdom, if the Kingdom is in Heaven? . . . the fowls of the air and all beasts that are under the earth or upon the earth and the fishes of the sea, these are they which draw you ; and the kingdom of heaven is within you, and whosoever shall know himself shall find it. Strive therefore to know yourselves, and ye shall be aware that ye are the sons of the Almighty Father ; and ye shall know that ye are in the city of God and ye are the city.*

3. *Jesus saith, A man shall not hesitate . . . to ask concerning his place in the Kingdom. Ye shall know that many that are first shall be last ; and the last, first ; and they shall have eternal life.*

4. *Jesus saith, Everything that is not before thy face, and that which is hidden from thee, shall be revealed to thee.*

* Grenfell and Hunt : *New Sayings of Jesus* (1904).

*For there is nothing hidden which shall not be made manifest ;
nor buried, which shall not be raised.*

5. *His disciples question Him, and say, How shall we fast,
and how shall we pray, and what commandments shall we
keep? Jesus saith . . . Do not . . . of truth . . . blessed
is he. . . .*

These ' Sayings ' do not give quite the same impression
of early date as those of Papyrus A. Some of them appear
to be derived from the Apocryphal Gospels, and one or
two are reminiscent of popular Greek philosophy. Nevertheless, there are scholars who believe that here we have
possibly ' one of the earliest attempts to write in connected
form an account of the Teaching of Jesus, and an attempt,
therefore, that dates back into the first or at least very early
in the second century.'

Several other isolated ' Sayings of Jesus,' of perhaps
even earlier date, have been found elsewhere. One of
them certainly deserves to be quoted : *Men must give an
account of every good word which they shall* not *speak.*

Of the ' Sayings ' in general, one may perhaps hazard
the remark that, though some of them sound sufficiently
thought-provoking to have been genuine utterances of the
Lord, yet it is notoriously easy to put memorable aphorisms
into the mouth of a beloved leader without paying too much
regard to the evidence that he actually spoke them. It is
impossible to be sure. But on this at any rate we can
build, that the writers of our canonical four Gospels have
included within them all the Sayings of Jesus which are
really necessary to Salvation.

CHRONOLOGICAL TABLE

DATE	THE WORLD	NEW TESTAMENT
B.C. 27	OCTAVIAN AUGUSTUS, Emperor of Rome.	HEROD THE GREAT, King of the Jews.
7	QUIRINIUS, Governor of Syria for first time.	Birth of Christ. Flight into Egypt.
4	Death of Herod. ARCHELAUS, Ethnarch of Judæa ; PHILIP, Tetrarch of Iturea ; HEROD ANTIPAS, Tetrarch of Galilee.	Return to Nazareth.
A.D. 6	QUIRINIUS, Governor of Syria for second time. Revolt of Judas.	Christ in the Temple, aged 12.
14	TIBERIUS, Emperor.	
26	PONTIUS PILATE becomes Governor of Judæa.	Ministry of Jesus begins. Aged ' about 30.'
29		The Crucifixion.
32		Conversion of S. Paul.
37	CAIUS (CALIGULA), Emperor.	
39	HEROD AGRIPPA I, King of the Jews.	
41	CLAUDIUS, Emperor. Agrippa builds part of Third Wall of Jerusalem.	
50		Earliest New Testament writing (Galatians ? S. James ?)
52	GALLIO, Proconsul of Achæa.	
53	HEROD AGRIPPA II, King of the Jews.	
54	NERO, Emperor.	
60		S. Paul's first Imprisonment.
61		
65		S. Paul's martyrdom.
68	GALBA, OTHO, VITELLIUS, Emperors.	
69	VESPASIAN, Emperor.	
70		Fall of Jerusalem.
79	TITUS, Emperor.	
81	DOMITIAN, Emperor.	
96	NERVA, Emperor.	
98	TRAJAN, Emperor.	
100		Latest of the Gospel (S. John's).
117	HADRIAN, Emperor.	
118		Jerusalem rebuilt as Ælia Capitolina.
131		Bar-Kochbar's Revolt.
133		Destruction of Ælia Capitolina.
138	ANTONINUS PIUS, Emperor.	
150		Earliest New Testament Papyrus (fragment of S. John).
161	MARCUS AURELIUS, Emperor.	
312	CONSTANTINE THE GREAT, Emperor.	
324	Establishment of Christianity.	
330		Earliest complete manuscript of the New Testament (Codex Sinaiticus).

SELECTED LIST OF BOOKS
Each section arranged in order of date

A. NEW TESTAMENT ARCHÆOLOGY IN GENERAL

W. Ramsay : *The Bearing of Recent Discovery on the Trustworthiness of the New Testament*, 1915.
C. M. Cobern : *The New Archæological Discoveries*, 1924.
Excellent Illustrated Articles in J. A. Hammerton's *Wonders of the Past* (1934) and *Story of the Bible* (1938),
and the *Proceedings of the Society of Biblical Archæology* (P.S.B.A.).

B. RELICS OF CHRIST (Chapter II)

W. Smith : *Dictionary of Christian Antiquities*, 1875.
F. W. Farrar : *Christ in Art*, 1896.
W. Lowrie : *Christian Art and Archæology*, 1906.
G. A. Eisen : *The Great Chalice of Antioch*, 1916.
C. M. Cobern : *The New Archæological Discoveries*, 1924.
J. R. Harris : *Glass Chalices*, 1927.

C. JERUSALEM AND PALESTINE (Chapters III, IV, V)

Palestine Exploration Fund : *Our Work in Palestine*, 1874.
C. Warren : *Recovery of Jerusalem*, 1875.
C. Warren and C. R. Conder : *Jerusalem*, 1884.
T. H. Lewis : *The Holy Places of Jerusalem*, 1888.
C. Conder : *Tent Work in Palestine*, 1895.
Bliss and Dickie : *Excavations at Jerusalem*, 1898.
C. C. Ganneau : *Archæological Researches in Palestine*, 1899.
W. Sanday : *Sacred Sites of the Gospels*, 1903.
C. W. Wilson : *Golgotha and the Holy Sepulchre*, 1906.
G. A. Smith : *Jerusalem*, 1907.
E. W. G. Masterman : *Studies in Galilee*, 1909.
Père Vincent : *Underground Jerusalem*, 1911.
Bent and Hussey : *Golgotha and the Garden Tomb*, 1911.
Palestine Exploration Fund : *Fifty Years' Work in the Holy Land*, 1915.
H. F. T. Duckworth : *Church of the Holy Sepulchre*, 1922.
R. Weill : *Excavations in Jerusalem*, 1925.
R. A. S. Macalister : *A Century of Excavation in Palestine*, 1925.
R. A. S. Macalister : *Excavations on Ophel*, 1926
Baedeker's *Guide to Palestine and Syria*, 1927.
J. W. Crowfoot and G. M. Fitzgerald : *Excavations in the Tyropœon Valley*, 1929.
G. Dalman : *Sacred Sites and Ways*, 1935,
and the *Palestine Exploration Fund Quarterly* (P.E.F.Q.).

D. THE TRAVELS OF S. PAUL (Chapter VI)

W. Ramsay : *Historical Geography of Asia Minor*, 1890.
R. Lanciani : *Pagan and Christian Rome*, 1893.
Murray's *Guide to Asia Minor*, 1895.
R. Lanciani : *Ruins and Excavations of Ancient Rome*, 1897.
W. Ramsay : *S. Paul the Traveller*, 1905.
W. Ramsay : *Cities of S. Paul*, 1907.
D. G. Hogarth : *Excavations at Ephesus*, 1908.
A. G. Mackinnon : *The Rome of S. Paul*, 1930.
R. Carpenter : *Ancient Corinth*, 1933.
R. Gunnin : *Historic Cyprus*, 1936,
and the *Journal of Hellenic Studies*, and the *Journal of Roman Studies*.

E. INSCRIPTIONS, PAPYRI, MANUSCRIPTS, ETC. (Chapters VII, VIII, IX)

B. P. Grenfell and A. S. Hunt : *Sayings of Our Lord* (1807).
B. P. Grenfell and A. S. Hunt : *New Sayings of Jesus*, 1904.
A. Deissmann : *New Light on the New Testament*, 1908.
A. Deissmann : *Light from the Ancient East*, 1910 (last ed. 1927).
G. Milligan : *The New Testament Documents*, 1913.
J. H. Moulton : *From Egyptian Rubbish Heaps*, 1917.
E. G. Hardy : *Monumentum Ancyranum*, 1923.
M. Van Rhyn : *Treasures of the Dust*, 1929.
H. I. Bell and T. C. Skeat : *Fragments of an Unknown Gospel*, 1934.
F. Kenyon : *Our Bible and the Ancient Manuscripts* (revised ed. 1939).

INDEX